DREAMING
TOGETHER

DREAMING TOGETHER

Explore Your Dreams
by Acting Them Out

JON LIPSKY

LARSON PUBLICATIONS

Library of Congress Control Number: 2008931442

Publisher's Cataloging-In-Publication Data
(Prepared by The Donohue Group, Inc.)

Lipsky, Jon.
   Dreaming together : explore your dreams by acting them out / Jon Lipsky.
   p. : ill. ; cm.
Includes bibliographical references and index.
   ISBN-13: 978-0-943914-59-6
   ISBN-10: 0-943914-59-0

1. Dreams. 2. Dream interpretation. 3. Acting--Psychological aspects. I. Title.

BF1078 .L57 2008
154.63   2008931442

Published by Larson Publications
4936 NYS Route 414
Burdett, New York 14818 USA

http://www.larsonpublications.com

17 16 15 14 13 12 11 10 09 08
10 9 8 7 6 5 4 3 2 1

Contents

List of Full Dreams

Acknowledgements

I would like to thank first and foremost, for his teaching and his friendship, Robert Bosnak, whose Embodied Dreamwork inspires this work. I am also indebted to my friend and colleague, Tim McDonough, for his innovative ideas about acting and imagery.

Many thanks to the actors who helped create the dream shows *Dreaming with An AIDS Patient* and *The Wild Place*, particularly David Zoffoli, Marshall Hughes, Susan Thompson, Kim Mancusa, and Kermit Dunkelberg and the dream ensembles of *Crossing the Water*, and *The Dream Project*. Thanks, too, to Steve Levine, Ellen Levine, and Paolo Knil, who provided an artist-in-residence position that enabled this work to proceed.

The theater department at Boston University, with the encouragement of Walt Meissner and Jim Petosa, has incorporated this work into its curriculum for many years, and the support is much appreciated. Thanks, too, to Paul Cash for his careful attention to this manuscript.

There are dreamers too numerous to mention who have inspired this work, but a few who must be acknowledged are: Maggie Simpson, Jordan Dann, Kathleen Donohue, Paula Langton, Ken Cheeseman, Bill Barclay, and Christa Lambertus. Likewise, my Dream Enactment workshop partners Kira Lallas, Margaret Ann Brady, and Jennifer Boyes-Manseau. To the many others who shared their dreams and their life-stories, much thanks.

Finally, I dedicate this book to my wife, Kanta, and my children Adam and Jonah, who share my waking dreams.

How to Navigate this Book

Dreaming Together is a guide for people who want to re-experience dreams by acting them out. Through enactment, we re-live our dreams and relate to dream characters as three-dimensional figures. This is a playful, interactive approach, rather than an analytic or psychological one. As such, it can circumvent some of the emotional baggage that often accompanies dream work. At the same time, Dream Enactment can go very deep and reveal ways our dream life intersects with, and enriches, our waking life.

This book is also for artists, particularly theater artists, who want to use dreams to further their training and hone their art. It outlines a method for getting in touch with the personal landscape of your imagination—exploring narrative, imagery, spatial awareness, relationship to audience, and ensemble techniques in depth. Ultimately, it creates a blueprint for a theater of dreams that offers a venue for sharing the passionate, provocative dramas of our inner lives.

The first section, Solo Dream Enactment, is directed towards the general reader—all who want to re-experience dreams in a physical way—and for groups of people who want to get to know one another better by sharing dreams. This level of Dream Enactment requires no more experience in acting than telling stories around a campfire or across a kitchen table.

The second section, Group Dream Enactment, is directed towards actors and non-actors alike. It's for people willing to collaborate with one another in acting out dreams as a way to re-encounter dream figures and re-enter the dream landscapes.

The third section, Making Dream Theater, is primarily for theater artists, theater students, and dream theater enthusiasts of any kind who find dreams sufficiently revealing to inspire the creation of formal and informal dramatic presentations devoted entirely to their enactment. In practice, I hope these divisions will be blurred by readers—that you will dip into sections that do not necessarily pertain to you, looking forward and back to get a better sense of both the fundamentals of this work and its more sophisticated aspects.

A personal introduction at the start of each section tells how I became interested in dreams and developed this method of Dream Enactment. In a fourth and final section, Waking Dreams, I suggest how this approach can enrich our daily life by fostering a new way of looking at everyday experience through the prism of our dream maker.

JON LIPSKY
West Tisbury, MA
November 2008

Prologue

THEATER OF DREAMS

An Overview

Our Own Shakespearean Stage

The eye of man hath not heard, the ear of man hath not seen, man's hand is not able to taste, his tongue to conceive, nor his heart to report, what my dream was.

—Bottom, *A Midsummer Night's Dream*

Some of us—I would say most of us—live a fairly humdrum existence. We may have our ups and downs—occasional adventures, momentary triumphs, simmering resentments—but most of our lives are lived in a habitual manner under ordinary circumstances. Often we are so busy, and so caught up in our routines, that we don't notice the emotional impact of our everyday life.

To put it another way: we may get angry with our boss, but we don't stick a knife in his back; we may fantasize about a woman on an elevator, but we don't start unbuttoning her blouse.

In dreams, we do.

In dreams, we live a life as rich and full as the *dramatis personae* of the Shakespearean stage. Our dreams are inhabited by killers and seducers, betrayers and enchanters, flying creatures and hideous monsters. And low-lifes, too, like the "rude mechanicals" in *A Midsummer Night's Dream*.

Plumbers and car mechanics populate our dreams; taxi drivers and shoeshine boys; our fat noisy neighbor and the scary old lady who lives next door. They are all there. Everybody. From the lowest of the low to the highest of the high. Not to mention our parents, our children, and our lovers in their many benign and malignant disguises.

Certain things that happen on the Shakespearean stage only happen to us in our dreams. Where else do we try to murder our brother, romance a queen, meet witches on the road or, like Bottom in *A Midsummer Night's Dream*, become the love toy of a Fairy Queen while sporting the head of an ass?

Dreams give us access to a range of experience that includes our mundane life but goes far beyond it. We experience in sleep the passions of a Cyrano, of a Hedda Gabler, of a Richard III. We become a thief, a movie star, a randy lover. We visit places as exotic as Prospero's Island, the forests of Elyria, and the castle at Elsinore.

At the same time, our dreams focus on more down-to-earth things: we have dreams of sitting on the toilet, dreams of cooking bacon in the kitchen, of fixing the engine of a car: everything from the sublime to the ridiculous. In dreams we drink, burp, fart, and bellow to rival John Falstaff. Dreams sometimes seem like they are making jokes; there are even dream puns.

Dreams expand our horizons and animate the ordinary. They make us feel the breadth of our desires and the passion we bring to everyday life. When we tell dreams and share these experiences with other people, we recognize a common humanity that goes far beyond the confines of our mundane existence.

In my experience, the immediate value of dreams doesn't come from explaining them, analyzing them, or following their overt or covert suggestions. It lies in re-entering them, living inside them, tasting and chewing them, until they become incorporated into the fabric of our waking hours. When we re-enact them we play "as if" they are really happening to us. Thus they "really happen" to us again and again.

On a practical level, this book provides a method for re-experiencing dream life as our own Shakespearean stage. Beyond this, though, is a larger purpose: to reanimate the ordinary through the imagery of dreams, and to bring the extraordinary back into our lives.

Take the following dream, for example, and imagine it as your own. What would it be like to live inside this dream over and over again by telling the story and acting it out? Playing all the parts, and entering all the images, you would become an ancient sailor, a mighty storm, and a young woman wildly steering a runaway boat whose Pilot has gone "night blind." It might even make you consider how, in your real life, you have been feeling out of control lately—as if your "pilot" is flying blind.

Christine's Night-Blind Boatman Dream

I am on a shore. I see a boat there. It is a very old wooden sailing boat. Inside sits a man with long dark hair. He seems ancient and holy like Jesus of Nazareth.

I like him and I want to get into the boat. As soon as I step on board, it leaves the shore and sails into the sea.

The sky is a golden orange. The water is still, reflecting the light.

Then the night comes in. And the darker it gets, the more the tempo of the boat picks up and accelerates. I see big buildings and big ships looming in the darkness along the waterstreet. Faster and faster we go, and I get scared because we are almost running into those grey shapes.

In a panic, I look to the man steering the boat next to me, hoping he will do something to slow us down. But he doesn't. He is totally indifferent to whether we live or die.

I try to tell him how dangerous this is— "Watch out! Look out!"—but he just shrugs and says: "Doesn't matter. I'm night blind."

Night blind! Omigod, I think. He can't see where we're going!

Suddenly, we drive very close to a huge ship and almost crash and I know I have to do something. Quickly, I get behind the boatman and put my hands on his shoulders. Very gently, I move him by his shoulders left and right as if to steer him. Like he is the steering wheel.

And it works. He puts up no resistance and is completely one with the boat. By steering him I can keep us on course. Through the night, I navigate the boat, swerving past the dark shapes without crashing into anything. It is very strenuous. I have to concentrate with all my might to peer into the thick darkness.

But finally the journey ends; the boat slows down and comes to the shore. I scold the boatman: "You know, it's very dangerous to drive through the darkness when you're night blind!"

Then I wake up.

What are dreams?

Dreams come to us in the shank of the night, in the light of dawn, in the lap of a nap. They come unbidden, on their own volition. Or they don't come at all, depending on their mood. We can sometimes coax them out, catch them on the fly, write them in a dream book, or tell them to our partner over coffee in the morning. But we can't make them up, or even remember them at will. They are, by nature, elusive creatures with their own volition, appearing or disappearing by their own whim.

Whether they have their own motivation or purpose—carrying insights, messages, or prophecies from our unconscious or from the gods—is a question I like to avoid, or at least dance around. My working premise is that just about *all* the assumptions people make about dreams are true—at least some of the time. Sometimes dreams seem to be random bits of daily flotsam and jetsam; sometimes they make deep emotional connections; sometimes they touch on our most intimate yearnings; and sometimes, for some people, they suggest paths for our life's journey.

My own experience with dreams is mainly poetic. When the imagery of my dreams resonates with my daily life, I find myself deeply moved, disturbed, or enlightened. Whatever your experience, this guide to Dream Enactment does not require you to have any particular take on dreams: you don't have to be a Jungian, or a Freudian, or anything like that. You just have to have a connection to your dreams that feels personal.

The only assumption basic to this work is that dreams are independent artifacts. Their imagery, character, narrative, and geography are not under our conscious control, and often don't obey either natural laws or societal norms. For all we know, dreams may have no "purpose" at all. Maybe they just *are*.

In any case, it's safe to approach them with this assumption, even if at times it seems that a particular dream is "talking" directly to us. It is this quality—that dreams are both part of us and apart from us—that makes them so valuable to anyone interested in their inner life, and to artists in particular.

How might we describe dreams, then, as independent artifacts, if we were, say, dream archeologists trying to evaluate what we find in the field? We would say first of all that dreams are fleeting. If we don't write them down, talk them out, or otherwise transfer them from short-term memory to long-term memory, we usually forget them.

Secondly, dreams almost always take place in a place. "I was sitting at my kitchen table . . ." "I was flying over my old childhood home . . ." "I was walking through a forest of white birch trees with patches of snow on the ground . . ."

On rare occasions, someone will dream that they are floating in outer space or surrounded by blackness; but this space or blackness usually has as palpable a quality as any other environment. Mostly, though, dreams have a specific location and, to the extent the dreamer can remember that setting, he can place himself back into the dream space and navigate within it.

Thirdly, dreams are experienced in the language and culture of the dreamer. When a Japanese woman dreams she is cooking a meal with her daughter, she is inevitably in a Japanese kitchen speaking Japanese. If the dreamer is fluent in more than one language or has a multicultural background, her dreams may sometimes come from one culture or the other, or from a mixture of the two, but rarely from a language or culture totally foreign to her experience. There are exceptions, of course, when dreams create exotic landscapes with tantalizing foreign words and customs; but even these dream fantasies are rooted in the fantasy notions of the dreamer's native soil.

If you listen to enough dreams of a particular person, it becomes clear that her dreamscapes carry their own individual signature, as specific and identifiable as her waking personality. For instance, my friend Juno, a quiet and somewhat somber poet, often has Gothic dreams with intricate and imposing architecture. My friend Jordan, on the other hand, tends to have transformational traveling dreams populated with fantastic creatures.

In other words, people seem to dream (or at least remember dreams) from their own peculiar vantage points. Our style of remembering dreams differs from person to person. Furthermore, our style of remembering dreams often differs from dream to dream. Sometimes we remember only a fragmentary image; sometimes we remember the dream as a disjointed story of oddly disconnected scenes; and sometimes as a coherent story that seems to lead towards a culminating event.

Finally, it should be said that dreams are rarely dreamy. They are usually very particular in detail: you are in your grandfather's apartment next to the old dumbwaiter, or swimming underwater with a shark that has peculiar patchy skin. There may be unusual juxtapositions in dreams—one minute you are in your grandfather's apartment, the next you are swimming with a shark—but they are rarely surreal, not at all like a Salvador Dali painting with its dripping time pieces. Some details may be remembered more in focus than others, but the details are specific, rarely generic. So it's worth your time to explore the details of the dream. The polka dots on an umbrella may be exactly the same as those on the polka-dotted umbrella you had when your parents divorced; the look in the eye of the hawk may be the same as the look in the eye of the teacher you revered in college.

The juicy stuff is in the details. [1]

Why tell dreams?

Dreams are personal, intimate, idiosyncratic. They bring up feelings unbidden. They invoke people and places that are dearest to us. And then they invoke people and places that seem totally inconsequential to us, and infuse them with emotional clout. Our most bitter or sweet moments are recalled and transformed in dreams, while other seemingly random moments are made equally frightening or enchanting. In short, our imaginations filter memory and experience through an emotionally charged image-maker that generates a personal response to ordinary and extraordinary things alike.

One obvious reason for telling dreams, then, is to get to know one another better, to create a window into our inner landscape. Telling dreams is an easy, safe way to share our intimate, emotional lives.

Of course, we could always decide to share intimate, emotional moments simply by telling one another our life stories. But how many of us would want to do that, particularly with strangers? Even with people we know fairly well,

---

1. This is why it's often rewarding to pay particularly close attention to any specific numbers, times, or dates in dreams. Usually dreams are vague on these matters, so when you have a dream that you must meet someone at 10:20 you might want to ask what happened, or what is supposed to happen, at 10:20 in real life, or if anything significant occurred on 10/20, that is, October 20, or if the series 10 . . . 20 . . . 30 . . . means anything to you.

we tend to keep our biographies fairly close to the chest. And even when we *do* decide to tell our life stories, they tend to be fairly well rehearsed, presented in a way that puts our best foot forward or shows our public face.

Dreams, though, by their very nature cannot be consciously prepared. Like a good poem or visual collage, they are revealing even without explicit biographical detail. The imagery speaks for itself. Luckily, we are not responsible for their content. The things we do in dreams are connected to our passions but not to our ethics, morality, and expected rules of conduct.

This makes them fun, intriguing, mysterious, and revealing, as in this dream I had a few years ago:

The Wild Men Dream

In this dream there are two wild men. They both have long, unruly, frizzy hair and rough, coarse, lumberjack-style shirts. One of them is tall and lanky, the other short and squat. The short squat one has a comb and stands behind the tall lanky one. He puts the comb through the frizzy dark hair of his wild companion, and starts blowing on it, making music. The music is the most beautiful, uplifting tapestry of sound. Not a buzzing, humming noise but something almost orchestral. When I woke up I couldn't remember the exact composition of the music but I could sense its soaring intricate architecture.

When I started to tell this dream to a dream group, much to my surprise, I broke into tears. I had thought the dream was simply about two strange creatures and their strange way of making music together. As I worked on it, though, I realized that this music-making reminded me of how I used to write songs with my good friend, Steve Cummings, who died prematurely a few years back. Steve and I looked nothing like these wild men, god knows; sometimes, though, our music came from a pretty wild place. Or, at least, *we* thought so.

Somehow, this dream gave me permission to vent my feelings about losing Steve. If someone would have asked me about Steve, I certainly would have said that I missed him. But, in a casual setting, I would never have shared with them the depths of my grief. The music in this dream made it unavoidable.

Telling dreams, then, is a way of sharing our humanity; happily, everyone can do it. No matter who you are, in sleep you are connected through emotionally charged imagery to your real-life experiences and the reflections of your imagination. Dreams are not fundamentally philosophical, theological, intellectual, or political, although elements of these things do creep in. On the most basic level, dreams are personal. This makes them extremely useful as a tool for helping people in any kind of group or gathering to let down their hair and reveal themselves.

When we do this in dream groups, surprising things happen. We discover that a seemingly uptight accountant has violent adventure dreams; a flamboyant artist dreams about his sixth-grade math teacher; a happily married and faithful housewife has exotic dream lovers.

It is almost impossible, telling dreams, to stereotype one another. Our dream lives are so rich we get to know each other in a deeper and more unpredictable way. While our social manners are still intact in the telling of our dreams, the dream imagery leads us both to the depths of our souls and to the heights of our flights of fancy. It even gives us clues as to how the minute details of everyday life have captured our imagination.

Working even for a short time on dreams, we quickly become aware of common threads. We all have flying dreams, wet dreams, dreams of being chased. Dreams connect us to one another because, even though they are idiosyncratic, they reflect our shared imagery and the experiences we have in common. We see ourselves in the dreams of others.

The telling of dreams, then, can be a formula for making the glue that binds groups together. Whether it is an acting ensemble, a social action group, an office staff, or almost any other kind of social gathering, dreams can help knit us together while cutting through layers of socialization and propriety to give us a window on our personal view of life.

Why act dreams?

A main reason to act dreams is that acting is playful. It cuts through some of the preconceptions, affectations, and expectations that often surround dream work. Its physicality allows conceptualization to take a back seat to the direct experience of the dream, and adds a healthy dose of fun to the serious task of exploring our inner life. The case for taking this approach can best be made, per-haps, by looking at some of the notions that often accompany dream work.

When I ask people about dreams, it seems that half of them say that they are rubbish and the other half that they are windows to the soul. Perhaps both are true.

Some scientific studies and much anecdotal evidence have contributed to the notion that dream images are the mental debris of waking life—that we process the overload of daily experience by randomly mixing a dream cocktail of this and that to make space in our mental computers for the next day's download. The dreams themselves have no meaning, purpose, or value, it is said. They're just random waste products of our mental activity.

In contrast, many people—particularly ancient and traditional cultures—attribute prophetic and visionary functions to dreams. In the Bible, after all, Joseph gains favor with Pharaoh by predicting seven years of plenty followed by seven years of famine from the Pharaoh's dream of fat and lean cattle. Black Elk of the Oglala Sioux tribe found his calling as a medicine man by dreaming of a broken hoop, which foretold the destruction of his people. Joseph Smith, the founder of the Mormon Church, had a dream which, it is claimed, correctly foretold his assassination the next day.

In modern times, too, in almost every group, you will find one or more people who have had dreams that changed their lives. Perhaps the dream gave them courage to take a new direction in their life, or to rethink their relationship to their husband or wife. A few will even claim to have had prophetic dreams that foretold some important event in their lives. In any case, for every person who feels that dreams are rubbish, there's another who swears by them.

And then there is the medical model. Since Freud, dreams have been a modern vehicle for therapy, a window into the psyche to help "cure" people of emotional trauma. As intimate, uncensored images from the Unconscious, dreams are said to give expression to fears, passions, instincts, and urges that are unexpressed in waking life. The analysis of dreams, in some circles, contributes to self-realization and the healing of past hurts. Perhaps this, too, is true of dreams, as many dreamers working with gifted therapists attest. Certainly, there is a great tradition in our culture, traced back to the ancient Greeks, of healing through dreams.

Whatever your take on dreams, it's safe to say that the scientific, prophetic, and medical traditions lay on dreams a lot of baggage. People tend to be either so skeptical of dream rubbish, so expectant of dream visions, or so afraid of dream therapy that they never allow themselves to accept their dreams at face value and re-experience them. Even if we enjoy dream work and feel nurtured by it, it is not uncommon to feel at times too vulnerable to dive so deeply, or to be exhausted by the emotional effort.

Most people, though, left to their own devices, enjoy their dreams or at least find them intriguing. Some of us even love them. We love them for no reason, just like we love the plants we grow in our garden. We love them not because of what they can do for us—though certainly some of them might nourish us or shower us with insights—but because they are ours. Dreams are the intimate creations of our dream weaver, the image-maker that is our imagination.

We take dreams personally. They *are* personal. No two people dream alike. No two people tell dreams in the same way.

Dreams are personal artifacts and, knowing this—if we can get past the baggage they carry—we can enjoy and experience them as our own creative emanations. Getting past the baggage, though, is no simple thing. As I have said: in every group you will find people who think dreams are rubbish, people who swear that they are windows to the soul, and people who believe they are vehicles for dealing with neurosis. Our expectations and preconceptions can get in our way even if we are dream junkies.

There also is a lot of resistance to dreams. In fact, it seems to be in the nature of dreams themselves to resist exposure. Dreams don't seem to want to be remembered, and people are often not eager to share them. They think they are either too insignificant— "Oh, it's just a dream"—or too loaded: "My god, I woke up screaming from a dream last night." So to get a group of people to come together and accept dreams at face value is no small charge.

My way of doing this is through acting, through storytelling, through theater. We say, "We're playacting; we're just putting on a play" to remind ourselves that dreams can be playful.

Some people have a resistance to acting, though, that's even greater than their resistance to dreaming. For them, the opposite approach may be helpful. Instead of saying, "Don't worry about the meaning of the dream, we're just putting on a play," we might say, "Don't worry about the acting, just tell us the story." The fact is that, when people tell their dreams—if they remember them vividly and recount them with animation—they act them out automatically. Without knowing it, they naturally go into storytelling mode, using voice and gesture and every trick of the actor's trade to convey their experience.

By playacting, we take some of the ponderous weight off dreams. We are not trying to cure our neuroses, or open windows to our souls, or get prophetic visions: we're just doing the grown-up equivalent of "show & tell." Even the emotional catharsis that can accompany the re-experiencing of dreams takes a back seat to our playmaking as we simply try to convey our experience through a dramatic medium. Of course, in the act of playacting, we may discover that we are moved, revealed, exposed, and inspired by our own dramatic discoveries.

Why Dream Theater?

A play *is* like a dream, as many artists have noted. For one thing, both are three-dimensional. They both always take place in a specific space. You can walk around in them. And what better place to enact dreams, with their quick shifts of scene, than the ever-shifting playground of a real or imagined theater set?

The traditions of theater also jibe well with the traditions of dreams as both have prophetic, visionary, spiritual, cathartic, and healing roots. The very baggage of contemporary dream work—the high expectations we put on it—can be incorporated effortlessly, almost invisibly, by our theatrical conventions. What is weighty, frightening, or inflated in a therapeutic situation can become dramatic, passionate, even entertaining in a play-acting context.

Neither is quite respectable either; both dreams and drama are socially suspect. In theater, as in dreams, we are confronted with situations that go beyond the realm of polite respectable behavior, with characters who are sexual, cruel, and wild. Indecent, inappropriate, impassioned actions happen in both arenas. And in both arenas, there is a shape-shifting quality that gives actors and dream characters a duplicitous, suspect reputation. Good dreams, like good theater, are unpredictable, confrontational, provocative, and crude. At the same time, plays, like dreams, are often created out of the mundane events of ordinary life to which we give emotional and symbolic weight.

In most "talking" dream groups, the depth of a dream is discovered by slowing everything down and spending lots of time with each image, particularly those images that pack the greatest psychological wallop. This is very effective in sounding the depths of the dream, but it raises a lot of expectations and resistance.

By enacting a dream, we avoid this burden by allowing the first telling to resemble a form of entertainment. We act it out as if we're sitting around a fire telling ghost stories. At first, whatever significance the dream has is secondary to the vividness of its imagery, its characters, its conflicts. Only by re-enacting the events over and over, does the deeper impact of the dream become clear. With each retelling, the intimate details are explored and the personal impact of the dream is re-experienced. This is a shaping process (similar to the rehearsal of any scripted play) which leads to greater clarity of detail and emotional depth. In that well-wrought theatrical dreamscape we can re-live the dream again and again.

For those who are inspired to explore their inner life in this way, Dream Enactment has the added benefit of providing an opportunity to practice the art of acting. While the details of this use of Dream Enactment are best reserved for Part Two, a few words here about what acting involves may be useful to the general reader.

Theater training is as much a vehicle for self-discovery as dream work. Unlike the musician with his oboe, or a painter with her canvas, the actor *is* the instrument. When the character cries, it is with the actor's tears; when the character falls in love, the actor's lips are kissing. Theater training is a discipline for creating and expanding emotional connections to body and voice, for discovering how we express ourselves in relationship to others, and for transforming into characters other than ourselves. Like dream work, it is, first and foremost, a personal exploration.

Performance, whether formal or informal, introduces a heightened reality; our senses become fully attuned to our surroundings; we become present in the moment while at the same time aware of everything that is going on around us. Eventually the performance of the dream becomes as moving and meaningful, if not more so, than the dream itself. In performance we experience a physical, three-dimensional dream of our dream.

Influenced by autobiographical material and laden with emotional moments, dreams naturally guide actors to make personal choices. This is important because, too often, untrained actors will make choices that are either divorced from their own experience or influenced by what they imagine a director or a playwright expects; too often they can't distinguish between authentic emotional discoveries and preconceived ideas about their role. Dreams are a laboratory, then, for discovering what it's like to drop into authentic emotional moments.[2]

The ability to trust one's own emotional experience is invaluable to everyone—particularly to actors. Playing Hamlet, you have to bring your own emotional impulses in line with the character's psychology, the playwright's intentions, and the director's vision. This involves making aesthetic choices. It's not always obvious, though, to an untrained person, what a personal aesthetic choice is. It takes practice to distinguish between appropriate emotional choices and superficial or self-indulgent ones. Dream Enactment provides a vehicle for building the confidence needed to personalize your work in this way.

Even if you have no intention of training yourself as an actor, by wearing the cloak of the actor in your dreams, you can learn a lot about what makes an impulse authentic and how to express your personal experiences in waking and dreaming.

---

2. In the progression of training, Dream Enactment, on the introductory level, provides a bridge between purely improvisational "opening up" exercises and work on text. On an advanced level, Dream Enactment is a practical tool for learning how to shape text by creating an action score. In terms of skills, formal dream presentations require actors to explore narrative, imagery, character, stylized movement, and relationship to ensemble, audience, and space.

Why dream together?

Theater is an act of collaboration: between actors and actors, actors and directors, actors and audience. It's a communal event. Even if we are not actors ourselves, when we *act* like actors we enter into this collaborative experience. By acting out dreams together we share our inner worlds with one another. Images that are private and universal, trivial and profound, are explored as a group; our dream stories are presented and witnessed through the lens of all the different sensibilities in the room.

There is a power in this. Working together creates an intensely shared experience. It helps us to see our personal moments in a more universal light. This is not just a theoretical idea. In working on dreams together, the empathy that you receive from others, and the empathy that you show towards others, can be deeply moving. You cannot act in someone else's dream without walking in their shoes. And if the people working on dreams with you are very different, if perhaps their backgrounds are opposite or antagonistic to your own, dreaming together can discover a path towards reconciliation. Imagine, for instance, a collaborative dream group made up of Palestinians and Israelis, blacks and whites, elders and youths, men and women. The very act of dreaming together implies a recognition of our collective humanity. Even groups that think they are homogenous—acting troupes, women's groups, high school wilderness experiences, corporate retreats—may discover much more diversity among their members by enacting one another's dreams.

Of the many benefits and challenges to "dreaming together," two are worth highlighting: the opportunity to encounter your dream figures, and the necessity of doing the work for someone other than yourself.

For instance, I had a dream of a young woman walking behind me, her head up against my back, following my footsteps perfectly, step by step, uphill, downhill, trusting me completely to lead her. The dream in memory was moving—I could feel how much she trusted me—but when I acted it out with a real woman behind me, something shifted. The first time we tried it, we could not get in step. We had to practice walking in sync over and over again. Finally, we got it, and in that moment I could feel how completely we were united, how the trust of the woman in my dream was based on a deep, abiding connection, like an ice skater, like an acrobat, in sync with her partner.

Presenting the dreams to an audience—*any* audience, even an imagined audience—also creates a shift in the dream work. Ultimately, it is in the dramatic presentation of the dream—an attempt to get others to experience what we experienced, to dream our dream—that we understand the nuances of the dream and how they resonate with universal images and themes. Our audience may be our fellow dreamers, or our family and friends; it need not be an actual theater audience. The act of presenting our work for others gets us out of our own self-absorption and makes us experience our dream in a larger context.

Most dream work is self-referential. We explore our dreams to find out more about our inner lives. This is problematic, though, because the biggest challenge in dream work is to get out of the ego, out of the "I" narrator, out of the idea that the person called "me" is the most important (or the *only* important) character.

By performing our dreams with and for others, we make a commitment to share what we've discovered. We are doing the work first and foremost to let others into our world. Our focus is not on having our own feelings (or, worse, indulging in them) but in communicating what happened. We do it for "them," not for us.

It is often thought that the therapeutic benefit of art comes from the artists' release of their pent-up emotions. While undoubtedly there is some truth in this, it pales beside the therapeutic benefit of moving other people. As the classical Greeks knew, the catharsis is for the audience. Seeing that you have moved your audience to laughter or tears seems to add value and meaning to your experiences. The joy or sorrow in your own life may not change because you share it with others, but it makes it feel somehow more worthwhile.

My friend Bill had the misfortune of losing his good friend Rob in a freak accident. Subsequently, Rob appeared to him in four dreams.[3] The presenta-

---

3. Actually, Bill had two friends die in freak accidents in the same time period, and dreamt of each of them twice. In performing these dreams, he decided to combine the images into one character for dramatic purposes. He felt intuitively that the dreams were part of the same series, that they were coming from the same place of loss, and that he could communicate this loss better by combining his friends into one dream figure.

tion of these dreams did not resolve the grief Bill was feeling. He still felt just as devastated. But the performance of his dream series became a kind of eulogy or requiem for Rob, one that honored their friendship and created a vehicle for other people to re-experience their own grief and sorrow. Perhaps this sharing is the best we can do to repair the world.

Bill's Visits from the Dead

On September 16, 2001, Robby fell off a cliff to his death. I should have been there—been the one to hold him as he died in that ravine.

But I have seen him since, four times, in my dreams.

First dream

In the first dream, I'm at a beach resort party looking out at a pool. Suddenly I realize I've forgotten something really important: today's the day Robby's gonna die. I think: Holy shit! I never said goodbye.

So I'm swimming, swimming for my life down the Mass Turnpike which has now become a four-lane pool. I slump back to my apartment. Exhausted, heavy, I turn a corner . . . There he is! There's Robby standing in his BoSox cap, hands in his pockets. His expression says it all: "I know you've been looking for me." And: "I know I'm dead."

Second dream

Then, again I'm swimming, swimming in a huge, flooded cabin room filled with water. I'm working my way through the room, when I see—a canoe? A canoe making its way towards me. It's Robby!

I pull myself up on the bow of the boat. "It's you. Oh my god. I can't believe it. I thought you were . . ."

He says: "It's me, Bill. I'm always with you. This is how we can see each other."

He means: "in dreams."

Third dream

The next time I see him I'm laying on top of him. Forehead to forehead. Chest to chest. Just lying there. Breathing . . . Breathing . . . I remember caressing his hair, pulling gently on his ear. Nothing matters, just the breathing. Breathing with Robby. Breathing . . .

Fourth dream

In the last dream, we're on the phone. Or maybe it's just a connection between worlds. We're shooting the breeze like we always did.

"Hey, Bill, how ya doin'?"

"Not bad, man. What's goin' on?"

"Not much. When am I going to see you again?"

(Pause)

"Robby, when am I gonna see you?"

(Pause)

He answers simply: "When you're at death's door."

Part One

TELLING THE DREAM STORY

Solo Dream Enactment

An Initiation Dream

Approaching middle age, I had a dream, which seemed, at first, of no great consequence.

Dream of the Shell & the Storm

I am twelve years old and floating in the bay on a rubber raft with Johnny L., my best friend then, whom I looked up to. The sky is clear; the water, calm. We are way out in the middle of the Great South Bay but have no fear because we consider ourselves experts on our rafts.

I slide off my raft and dive down to the bottom. It's not too deep. I see in the white sand a perfect little shell, the kind a hermit crab would hide in. I pick it up, pop to the surface, and show it to Johnny L. with great excitement. The color is ordinary—white with brown flecks—but the shape seems exquisite to me. It feels like a little treasure.

Johnny stares at it with a kind of blank look; it's just a plain, ordinary shell to him.

At that moment, the wind picks up. The sky turns dark and it looks like it's going to storm. I start swimming to shore as the waves pick up. Johnny has disappeared and it is just me alone out in the sea. By the time I get to the beach the sky has turned black and there are ominous lightning flashes. Up in the sky, towering above me, I see a three-pronged fiery bolt and feel the awesome power behind those thunderheads.

I see myself from a distance running along the beach, looking for shelter. There is a tremendous clap of thunder and flash of lightning; I am caught mid-stride in that terrible glare. As in a freeze-frame, my image is captured by that lightning bolt, a frozen moment in time. In that flash, I am petrified and illuminated.

This was the first dream I presented to my first dream group. I remember the event vividly. After I had finished telling the dream, I felt that I had totally failed; that my dream was really stupid; that everyone else had interesting dreams, everyone but me. What's more, I felt all churned up inside, frightened by the depths of my feelings, and ashamed that everyone could see what an emotional mess I was.

Of course, no one in the group said anything to me to make me feel this way. It was just what I felt, and I hid these feelings, even from myself.

I went to a café bar, really upset. I downed a couple of glasses of cheap wine and started writing furiously in my dream notebook, unaware of why the telling of this dream had brought up so much stuff. Over the years I've thought about this dream a lot. And it has seemed more and more appropriate that it should be the initial dream of my dream work.

I didn't know it then, but, just as in my dream, I had taken a dive into my depths. Dream work, I would learn, *is* like diving; and the deeper you go, the more pressure you feel—psychic pressure, of course, but pressure nonetheless. If you listen to enough dreams, you can begin to feel the pressure even from the outside as a listener. You can feel how deep the dreamer has gone into the depths of their dream by the pressure of the atmosphere in the room.

But I didn't know that then. I just felt the pressure. Sitting in the bar, I was aware only that this seemingly simple dream had shaken me to my core, leaving me exposed, scared, and ashamed. Why, I didn't know. It never occurred to me then that it might be the images themselves that had touched me so deeply.

If I had been more savvy about dreams, I might have written down a list of what had happened to cause my reaction: diving had happened; a precious object had been found and shown; a friend had been unimpressed; a dramatic storm had come up; a flash of light had illuminated and petrified me. At the time, though, I wasn't clear-headed enough about dreams to recognize the obvious: perhaps it was the series of images that had brought up my storm of unexpected emotions.

So, I wrote in my notebook the one thing I did know, though I hadn't admitted it to myself until that moment. I had chosen this dream over all the other dreams I could have told for a questionable reason: I was trying to impress people, or at least fascinate them with one of my images, the three-pronged lightning bolt. I was aware, having read enough mythology, that this was the shape of the Trident, the power object wielded by Poseidon, the Greek god of oceans and earthquakes. And I thought: "Ah, here's something archetypal that my dream group can really chew on." With a smattering of Jung under my belt and a flair for the theatrical, I was drawn to the majesty of this symbolism. I liked the idea that little me could have such a big dream image. I even liked the melodrama of the storm.

The leader of our group was Robert Bosnak, a psychoanalyst who had trained at the Jung Institute in Zurich. He had a private therapy practice but was also interested in teaching people how to work with dreams in groups.

His main technique for this work was to slow things way down. Often we would work on a single dream for the entire two hours. The dreamer would be asked not only to tell the dream, but to re-enter it imaginatively: not just to see the pictures, but to go back inside the dream space.

Once inside, Robbie and the group would ask questions of the dreamer beginning with the most banal and matter-of-fact details: "What was the temperature of the water?" "How did the rubber raft feel on your skin?"

Sometimes the questions were more personal: "How did it feel to be caught in the storm?" Often, though, the questions would simply serve the purpose of keeping the dreamer inside the images, coaxing him or her to picture the dream moments over and over again in order to answer all the questions.

So we began the exploration of this dream with the most ordinary questions. What was the temperature of the water? Cool, refreshing. What was the weather like? Clear skies, balmy clouds. How did the rubber rafts feel? Secure: We feel like expert raft riders, who fearlessly ride big surf waves on our rafts.

And of course I spent what seemed a huge amount of time describing this shell, which seemed so special to me, frustrated that, no matter how hard I tried, I never could seem to convey its precious charm.

But then Robbie asked one of his favorite questions— "What's it like?" What's it like to show this shell to your best friend?

The first thing I thought of was my collection of china animals. When I was very young—six? eight?—I began collecting china animals . . . penguins, horses

. . . and these were very precious to me. When I showed them to someone I always expected them to love them as much as I did. They had (and still have) an honored place in my china cabinet. So showing this shell is like showing one of my china animals.

"And what's that like?"

Well, as I thought about it, it felt a bit like opening night of one of my plays as the curtain is about to go up revealing my creation.

Inside the dream, in the water, popping to the surface, I could feel this mixture of joy, excitement, and anticipation as I revealed the treasure I had pulled up from the depths. I was hoping, I was expecting that Johnny L. would treasure it as much as I did. I wanted him to see what a great thing I had found. But he didn't. He thought it was just an ordinary shell, not a treasure.

Switching points of view—another favorite Bosnak maneuver—I could feel, looking at myself through Johnny L.'s eyes, that I was still his friend, that we were still on this adventure together, but the shell was no big deal.

"And what's *that* like?"

Well, of course it's like the audience reaction on opening night when, even if almost everyone likes the play, even if most of the people are moved by it, not everyone appreciates it, some don't understand it, and maybe even some people just find it (worst of all) ordinary, nothing special, just another play.

"And what's that like?"

Sitting in the bar writing in my dream book, I realized that it's very much like telling your first dream in front of your first dream group—full of excitement and anticipation—and feeling that it is received, not as a treasure, but as no big deal, just another dream.

Hmmm . . .

And then the storm comes up. It doesn't feel like the showing of the shell to Johnny L. causes the storm. But that is what happens next—the two events are somehow connected. The dark clouds roll in, the waves kick up—lightning! thunder!—a sudden flash, and, as I swim for shore, high in the sky appears a tremendous electric bolt in the shape of the god's Trident.

"So what's *that* like?"

Initially, I had thought it was pretty dramatic. But as Robbie and others in group asked questions about this three-pronged flash, the more and more it sounded melodramatic, full of "sound and fury, signifying nothing."

Not that anybody said this. It was just how I felt, hearing my own voice describe these clouds, these flashes of light—what seemed impressive, a dream treasure, was really just all puffed up.

Sitting in the bar, shaken by the experience, I realized that this storm was still raging in me: a melodramatic storm, to be sure. What had happened, really, was that all this emotion felt like some kind of foam, insubstantial, almost a cartoon. I felt exposed, as if my feelings were fake, as if I had failed to say anything of substance.

And this made me afraid and ashamed. I don't know why it brought up so much fear and shame, but it did. The fact that I could not present a dream of any substance made me feel insubstantial, false, fake. My little treasure of a dream was not only unimpressive, it was without value. Or so it seemed.

Except for one thing: that lightning bolt had caught me in its flash, had captured me like a photograph, in a frozen moment of time.

"What's it like?" "What's it like?"

In my dream notebook, I had written down: "In that flash I am petrified and illuminated."

"Petrified." "Illuminated." When I first wrote these down, I had meant that I was petrified like an insect in amber, frozen in time, and that I was illuminated by the flash in the darkness and revealed in mid-stride.

But as I looked at these words and as I worked on this dream subsequently, it became clear that they had double meanings. Clearly, the telling of this dream petrified me, scared me by how much I felt revealed by it. At the same time, in some strange way, this dream, my initiation dream, was illuminating, showing clearly, starkly, in vivid relief, some aspect of the alchemy of my being.

Since that time, having worked on many dreams myself and heard many dreams told and enacted, I have more understanding and compassion for my Shell & Storm Dream. Over and over I have experienced how I dive down to my depths to find my treasures, my precious things, how I try to show these things of value to those I admire—hoping they will find them just as valuable. Storms accompany these actions, melodramatic, full of sound and fury. But while it feels like this process is signifying nothing, that's not quite true. While it is petrifying, revealing me in stark relief, it is, at the same time, illuminating, opening me up to unexpected revelations.

Even telling this dream now, imagining it revealed in this book, brings up some of those old feelings. The only difference is, I've been here before and I know the emotional territory. The storm is not so grandiose; the lightning not so petrifying. And even the little shell of a dream is not so precious. It's one of many dreams that weave a portrait of my inner life.

In any case, this is how dream work works. You tell a dream and relive it. In reliving it, you re-experience it, sometimes discovering new things, sometimes uncovering depths of feeling you didn't know you had. The dream cooks. You hold up the images again and again, looking at them from different points of view, and new connections are made. The dream becomes a foreign country you can visit until, over time, you learn to navigate within it and discover how its scenery and customs reflect on the activities that go on in the land you inhabit in the daylight hours.

This book, then, is a special kind of cookbook: how to cook dreams by enacting them.

Weaving Tales

Entering the dream story

The first step toward re-experiencing your dreams is to re-enter the dream story. We do this all the time when we wake up in the morning and relate to our partner or best friend the wild things that happened in the night. But often this is done from a distance, from a daytime perspective, remarking on the strange characters and weird environments, but not really feeling their presence. An alternative, which is much more satisfying and enlightening, is to enter fully into the story as if it were happening to you all over again.

Telling dreams at the kitchen table

The easiest way to enact dreams is to avoid the notion of "acting" altogether and simply tell them as you would in a café, or at the kitchen table. Tell the dream any way you want. Acting will happen. It's inevitable. If the dreams have strong emotional moments or vivid characters or striking images, you will intuitively and instinctively start to use gesture and expression and tone of voice to convey the story.

For instance, when my friend, Anna, at a café first told me her dream about "The White Bull" (see p. 155) she acted it out without even thinking about it. Her eyes naturally got wide with fear when she described the bull, and her voice dropped to a lower register when she related what the bull seemed to be thinking:

"Since you are so scared I'll put you over the fence." And very gently he lifts me over the fence and places me down outside the field.

Demonstrating how the bull lifted her up, she automatically put two fingers on her forehead as a sign of horns, and showed how gently the bull lifted her by a small nodding gesture.

I look back and in the place of the bull is a tall handsome boy of twenty. Somehow I know he is my son.

In the café, when she tells me this part of the dream her eyes tear up, her voice quavers a little. Anna doesn't have a son in real life; the depth of her longing for a child appears without effort or affectation. It's simply how she feels about this image.

Good acting is being present in the moment. Like Anna, if you can simply re-experience your dream while telling it, you will naturally "act" the way you feel.

This way of telling dreams—as if at a café or at the kitchen table—is a particularly good way to start dream work in a group that is made up of people who don't think of themselves as actors. By seeing the natural way people in conversation strike poses, make faces, change voices to convey what happened, it becomes clear that everyone is an actor, even if they have no experience.

All the same techniques that are used to tell a story at the kitchen table can be used for more theatrical presentations. Watching how people naturally tell stories is a first step towards figuring out techniques for Dream Enactment.

There is a great benefit in starting off with this kind of dream telling. For one thing, everyone can do it and you can't get it wrong. Whatever happens, happens. But more than that, it demystifies the telling of dreams and makes it a natural thing to do.

It bears repeating: people bring to dreams all kinds of baggage. Some find dreams hopelessly obscure, while others are scared they will reveal too much. Whatever the preconceptions, most people when they hear a series of dreams recognize that they are funny, moving, revealing, and common to us all. The baggage naturally drops away.

People tend to devalue their dreams because they forget them easily or only remember inscrutable fragments. Upon hearing other people's dreams, however, even the most jaded dreamer recognizes that, at least for other people, dreams—even dream fragments—seem to be meaningful. Often, the telling of dreams "at the kitchen table" will stimulate people to remember more of their dreams.

Finally, by starting off with this laid-back, conversational style of telling dreams, the focus can be on the dream material itself and its relationship to the dreamer, not on performance challenges that might be intimidating. It puts us in the land of dreams without a lot of melodrama and reminds us that dreams are ordinary reflections of our inner life. Hopefully, it also introduces the idea that dreams are fun to tell and listen to. Any group sharing a bunch of dreams with one another is sure to be moved by the personal feelings evoked by the dream figures, and sure to crack up laughing over the crazy, delightful juxtaposition of images.

Telling dreams around a campfire

Another easy and unimposing way of getting into Dream Enactment—but one which adds a little more theatricality—is to tell dreams as if you were storytelling around a campfire. That is, you tell your dream in the same way you would tell children a fairy tale or a ghost story: acting out the main actions and playing all the parts. The story of *Goldilocks and the Three Bears* requires that you put on a different posture and voice for Papa Bear, Mama Bear, and Baby Bear. In the same way, you would tell your dream dramatically setting all the scenes, portraying all the characters, and acting out all the actions.

> *It is a dark and a gloomy night. All the little children are tucked in bed, when suddenly they hear, oh! heavy footsteps on the roof—boom! boom! boom!—and a deep voice calling, "Who stole my big thumb?!"*

In this fairy tale of *The Giant Who Lost His Big Thumb*, you would naturally make a dark and gloomy voice to describe the night, make an innocent kid voice to curl up safe and snug in bed, and, with your face, act surprised and scared by the noise on the roof, while your voice and stomping feet act out the *boom! boom! boom!* of the giant's step.

In the same way, you can act out dreams in storytelling fashion.

Here's a dream of Anna's after she had become familiar enough with Dream Enactment that she felt comfortable to get up and demonstrate some of the narrative.

Anna's Bear Dream

I am in my car and see, in the back seat, a cushion, like the Indian prayer cushion I have just started using for meditation. As I step out of the car, I see, where the cushion sat, a baby bear. Suddenly, I hear a roar. It's the mother bear, very fierce, bellowing behind a heavy wooden barn door. I want to run but there's no escape. The mother bear breaks down the door, but instead of attacking me, she begins to turn white, like a statue, like marble, but very delicate as if her fur were covered with hoar frost. When she is totally white, the mother bear, in formal oriental fashion, bows deeply to me. I bow deeply to the mother bear.

In telling this dream, Anna, who had been sitting at a table, felt compelled to get up in order to show how the mother bear bowed. She felt compelled, too, to push through an imaginary door to show the power of the mother bear to break through. These actions seemed all the more necessary because Anna is Swiss and felt she could not convey the images to her English-speaking audience with sufficient precision without getting up on her feet and showing the action.

This suggests the level of theatricality this form of Dream Enactment entails. It is as if you are telling the dream to someone who does not quite catch the nuances of your language—a child, perhaps, or a foreigner. So you tell the simple and descriptive parts in an ordinary manner, but the strange and powerful parts you act out on your feet to make sure your listener gets it.

The advantage of this technique is that everyone has experienced this kind of storytelling and can imagine how to do it even if they are shy about it. It also begins to establish the kind of imagery that will be basic to the embodiment of all dreams: environments, characters, objects, and actions. Groups that are shy or inexperienced as actors will settle into more dramatic Dream Enactment by warming up to it through this kind of campfire storytelling.

If dreams were, indeed, fairy tales, we might leave it at this: just tell the stories and enjoy them for their odd, vivid narratives and images. But dreams are more than this. They often seem to resonate on a personal basis. They are connected in a mysterious (and sometimes not-so-mysterious) way to our waking life. And their imagery often seems to have layers of meaning, like a good poem or painting.

To get to the more intricate and powerful aspects of dreams, we need a form of enactment that is more sensitive to the nuances of dream life. We need to fully embody the images as if we are both telling it and, at the same time, re-living it. From outside the dream, we are narrating, relating the images to one another and to our waking life. From inside the dream, we are re-experiencing the events, not just from our own point of view but from every point of view the dream offers.

This is more complex than storytelling at the kitchen table or around the campfire, and requires a number of different steps. The following pages lead you through a process that includes choosing a dream; warming up to dreams; working physically and vocally with dream settings, characters, objects, and actions, and culminates in informal solo dream presentations.

Choosing a Dream

Fresh dreams! Fresh dreams! A-live, a-live-o

How do you choose a dream? After all, they don't come with critical rat-ings—four stars, like the movies. To get comfortable with dreams—telling them as if around the campfire or kitchen table—it doesn't really matter what dream you tell. Choose whatever intrigues you: your childhood flying dream or a re-occurring chase sequence.

It does matter, though, what dream you choose to fully enact. For one thing, you will have to live with it for a while, as you explore it and prepare it for presentation. More significantly, if you haven't done this before, it will be an initiation dream, whether you like it or not. I don't mean that it has to have great significance for you or that it needs to be an extraordinary dream. I simply mean that it will initiate a connection to dreams on a more physi-cal, visceral level, so you might consider how you want to enter into this new relationship.

So, how do you decide?

For some people, the choice will be obvious: there's a recent dream you've been dying to tell for weeks now, or one from a critical period in your past that has always inspired or haunted you. Both would make good choices because there is a strong personal connection.

But if the choice isn't obvious or there are too many choices, your best guide is how vividly you can remember a dream. Can you place yourself *inside* the dream, feeling again what it's like to be part of that landscape? Can you feel the quality of the environment? Can you feel it in three dimensions as a place where you can live and move about? It's okay if some of the dream is vague or fragmentary, but at least a central element of the dream should be physically tangible, as if you can reach out and touch it.

To put it another way: if you *can't* remember the dream vividly, if it's only a bunch of words on a piece of paper, or a story you remember like some kind of slide show or historical artifact, I would avoid it. We're going to try to explore the images from *inside* the dream; so if you can't get inside, make another choice.

Choose, instead, a dream you have some strong emotional connection to: your eighth-grade girlfriend who beckons to you with a glance, the warm ocean swells that rock you like a baby, the face of a madman who wakes you in terror. Something in the dream should attract you or repel you, fill you with calm, joy, lust, fear, fury, helplessness, or some other feeling that returns again and again when you re-enter the dream. These feeling tones will help you re-enact the dream with passion and conviction, and will often be a guide to how the dream relates to your waking life.

A word sometimes associated with special dreams is "numinous." That is, certain dreams seem to have a special quality, a powerful aura, a deep resonance. By all means choose one of these dreams if you can.

Dreams can be sneaky, though. There are times when you can't put your finger on the feeling of a dream. And there are times when a dream seems very ordinary only to prove to be more profound.

One of my favorite dreams in this category was a pizza dream of a young actor named Bobby.

Bobby's Pizza Dream

I am in my kitchen and there's a pizza on the kitchen table divided into eight sections and each section has a different thing I love: anchovies, black olives, pepperoni, things like that. And I'm starving, so hungry my mouth is watering. I can't wait to dig into this pizza. The only trouble is, my hands are tied. I don't feel ropes or anything but somehow I can't get my hands out from behind my back. I try and try but it's like my hands are paralyzed or something—they just can't reach around to pick up the pizza. And I feel really mad that all that good food is going to go to waste.

When Bobby first told this dream, he thought it was silly and banal. But the more we worked on how paralyzed he felt, how his "hands were tied," the more it resonated with the weight problem he had as a teenager and how mad he was about the way his family tried to shame him into dealing with it.

So don't discount a dream just because it seems ordinary on the surface. Dreams about ordinary things—your annoying kid brother, shopping at the mall, fixing your bicycle—can be the best dreams to work with. You don't need fantastic creatures or passionate encounters to make a dream meaningful. Daily life in dreams can be magical too.

Whenever someone says, "Oh that's a stupid dream," or "I had a dream last night but it's not very interesting," I get interested. They are often the most evocative dreams.

The one thing you *don't* want to do is pick a dream for its entertainment value. Even though this is Dream Theater, and theater *is* entertaining, if you pick a dream because you think it will amuse or amaze your audience, you are starting off on the wrong foot. The temptation will be great to push the dream in the direction you think will amuse or amaze, and you will perhaps avoid some subtler aspects of the dream that you have overlooked. Similarly I wouldn't pick a dream that you think you understand. You already have a preconceived notion about what the dream is about and are therefore less likely to be open to discoveries.

For this reason, I would pick a dream that is very recent—a fresh dream, hot off the press, so to speak. As long as you can recall it vividly and feel its resonance, last night's dream is a good choice. For one thing, it's more likely with last night's dream that you will discover new things about it in the process of exploring it. You won't have gone over it so many times that it's already mined for all its riches. What's more, with a recent dream, you'll be more likely to associate dream images with what's going on right now in your real life. Not that every dream contains strong associations with daily life, but many of them do. Sometimes seemingly trivial events trigger the images in your dream, and these associations inform those images, making them richer and more specific.

On the other hand, a dream from two months ago that has been haunting you or delighting you may trump last night's dream because the earlier dream is so evocative. But, all things being equal, the rule of thumb should be that the more recent dream is preferable to the older dream.

Some people don't remember whole dreams. They remember only frag-ments. Or they remember dreams as a series of snapshots, not a moving picture. Others have the opposite problem: they have epic dreams which go on and on in a seemingly endless series of transformations. Both kind of dreams—frag-ments and epics—are fine to use for enactment. If the fragment is vividly remembered and emotionally evocative, it is preferable over a longer dream that has evaporated. Similarly, an epic dream should not be rejected just because it's long and difficult to do. If the material calls to you, it's worth doing. It may take more time to tell, but so what?

If you remember only a fragment of a dream, tell all the details of that fragment. If you choose an epic dream, work on each part separately but *don't* eliminate parts of the dream. As much as possible, maintain the integrity of the dreams by neither eliminating details nor making up stuff.

Some say that dreams are windows to the soul. Whether you buy that or not, *acting* as if dreams are windows to the soul can help you determine which dream to tell. Ultimately, the main criterion for choosing a dream should be: Does it resonate with you on a meaningful level?

Letting the dream choose you

For some people, choosing a dream, particularly a first dream, can be confusing or intimidating. To take the burden off your shoulders, it can be helpful to let the dream choose you rather than the other way around. Imagine yourself surrounded by your dreams, especially your recent dreams; you might even place them, in your imagination, around the workshop space or other venue where you are working. Then see which dreams call out to you, as if they have their own agenda. Some might call out because they would be so much fun to do, or because they would be really moving. Others, though, might call out something quite the opposite, like: "Don't choose me: I'm completely incom-prehensible" or "Don't choose me: I'm much too difficult" or even "Are you out of your mind! I would be so embarrassing!" These might be just the dreams you should choose. Some dreams attract, some dreams repel. Sometimes the ones that resist you the most are the most fruitful.

When to choose childhood dreams

People who do not remember their dreams very well will gravitate often towards childhood nightmares as a source of dream material. There is nothing inherently wrong with this—the nightmares are often still vivid and emotionally charged—but they do have their limitations. The main limitation is that childhood dreams hold few surprises. If the dream is remembered into adulthood, it has been worked over in memory many times. It is a well-plowed field. Also, while the issues that generated the nightmares may still resonate, they are often well-buried or reasonably resolved.

Contemporary dreams, then, are generally preferable to childhood dreams for Dream Enactment. They are more open to discoveries and their issues are generally more unresolved. If you *do* choose a childhood dream, though, it's helpful to say at what age you had the dream and anything that was going on at the time that might resonate with the images. It's also helpful to see if you can remember a childhood dream that was *not* a nightmare. These are often richer and more surprising.

The very limitations of childhood dreams, however, can be of benefit if a dreamer is reluctant to reveal stuff about her current life, or if the group is young or inexperienced. Childhood dreams are generally shorter and feel, for many people, safer. For this reason they can be used as an introduction or a warm-up to acting out more recent dreams.

For example, here is one of my childhood dreams that still haunts me.

The Apocalyptic Sun Dream

I am about ten years old, standing at the window of my bedroom on the fifteenth floor of our apartment building in New York City. The sidewalk below is completely empty of people and no cars move in the street. A sickly yellow light shines from a cold sun that hangs like a death's head over the avenue. By the remorseless, hollow quality of the light I know it is The End of the World.

Every time I relate this dream, apocalyptic images in the real world flash through my mind: the mushroom cloud, the 9/11 tragedy, the burning rain forest. Childhood dreams can still pack a wallop in adult life.

What if you don't remember your dreams at all?

Take a nap. Nap, again.

Really, naps in the middle of the day incubate dreams. The sleep is light and the waking gentle. This is often the right time to capture dreams if your night dreams are elusive.

Another way is to keep a little beep clock by your bed and set it for 4:00 in the morning. The sound should be gentle so it won't jar you awake. Keep a little night-light there, too, right next to your dream journal so you can just roll over and start writing. Don't forget to have the book open and the pen ready. Any little excursion out of bed might provide an excuse for the dream to evaporate.

Remember, what you are trying to do is to move the dream from short-term memory to long-term memory. Writing it (and reading it over in the morning) will help to make this transfer. It helps, too, to start by scribbling down the key images in the dream—particularly the key people, places, objects, and actions—even before you write the whole thing out.

For instance, for my Initiation Dream (*see p. 33*) I might have first jotted down:

Rafts, Johnny L., dive, shell, storm, trident, lightning flash.

If you don't have a pen handy, saying these words aloud until you can put your fingers on something to write with may prevent the dream from disappearing.

A word of warning: don't be discouraged or surprised if, at first, you just remember a fragment of a dream. In fact, if you haven't been remembering your dreams, it's more than likely that you will *only* remember fragments in the beginning. But even fragments can be very resonant and insightful.

I had a dream years ago that was quite long and intricate, but when I awoke all I remembered was a fragment: the image of a tablet. It was a little like the Ten Commandments tablet only smaller. On it were chiseled out the words: "All you asses be gone and be faces." I woke up laughing and have been meditating on that sentence ever since, particularly at long boring meetings where the mantra echoes inside my head: "All you asses be gone and be faces!"

If you *still* don't remember your dreams after using these techniques for a week or so, you might try a little trick. When you wake up, write down how you feel and any associations you have to that feeling: *Anxious. Work. Exam. My brother is smarter.*

Don't make up a dream. But assume the feelings and thoughts you have on waking are linked somehow to your dream weaver. This is a way of tuning your mind to the images that lurk just below consciousness when you awaken.

Along the same lines, one other little trick is to tune your mind just before sleep to the dream frequency by taking yourself on a mental journey. As you lay in bed getting sleepy, try to clear your thoughts and imagine that you are traveling along a favorite terrain. Perhaps you're flying over snow-capped mountains, or driving through the desert, or skimming over a chain of lakes. The important thing is to try to take this journey without controlling what you see next. Let the images come to you, rather than conjure them up by an act of will.

This state of seemingly effortless imagination simulates the intuitive, associative stream of consciousness experienced in dreams. Often you will find yourself controlling the story, and often the journey itself will run out of steam, leaving you with the chatter of thoughts that fills our waking hours. However, once in a while you'll find yourself having a kind of structured daydream which makes you more receptive to your nighttime dreams. The more you do this, the more effective the technique becomes. And even if it doesn't help you remember your dreams, it's a delightful way to quiet the daily chatter and prepare yourself for sleep.

A word about keeping a useful dream notebook: start with a list of key images. You want to be able to find interesting dreams without reading your whole dream book cover to cover. Your list of key images at the top of the page should help you map your dreamscapes. And for even quicker reference, you might want to give each dream a title—The Shell & the Storm, for instance, or The Night-Blind Boatman, or The Tempting Pizza.

With a title and key words for reference, you should be able to look through your dream notebook at the end of the day and recall most of the images from the past week. By making this a habit just before bed every night, you can start to follow the progression of your dreams and watch them weave their way through your imaginative life. Some people even claim to be able to incubate particular dream images or themes before they go to sleep at night. This never works for me, though, and I'm suspicious of any attempt to control the content of dreams, since the charm of them is their autonomy.

It is my experience that the remembering of dreams comes and goes in waves. For a while, I remember nothing, then a fragment, then more fragments, then a whole dream. Suddenly, I'm remembering multiple dreams every night and the recording of them becomes tedious and exhausting. I feel overloaded with images. Then I become selective about which images to write down. And I start remembering less and less. Until I'm only remembering fragments. Then, for a while . . . nothing. My dreams seem to go underground until the whole cycle starts again.

Warming Up to Dreams

The dreamer as explorer

The crucial step in actually re-enacting dreams, beyond merely telling the dream story, is to fully embody the images physically and vocally. This involves finding the right posture, gesture, movement, tone of voice, and rhythm to bring the images to life—something easier said than done. It is less demanding (and less affecting) to tell what happened in a dream than to show it. To show what happened passionately, with full dramatic effect, we need the full range of body and voice. And to evoke *all* the dream images, we're going to have to stylize many of them to convey their essence.

In the dream below, for instance, how would you convey the power of the whale's tail, or the impish look in his eye? Using only your body and voice, how would you embody and show the terror, the fun, and the sexual undercurrent?

Greta's Whale Dream

I am swimming in the ocean, which is warm and calm. I sense there is something stirring in the deep. Suddenly I feel a powerful presence slip between my thighs and—yeeooow!—it lifts me up high above the water. It's the tail of a whale. A gray whale with a sparkling eye. It's terrifying. Let me down! But then . . . then I begin to enjoy it. It's kind of fun. And I can sense the whale thinks so, too. I can see his eye and it's full of mischief. Let's have some fun, he thinks, as he flips me up high over his head. Wow, what a ride![4]

Like the ecstasy of the joyride on the whale's tail, some dream moments seem almost inexpressible because they are too large to convey. Other dream moments are too subtle, like the look in the whale's eye.

Some dream moments seem too ordinary: a phone conversation about money with your mother. Others seem to defy expression: you know that your best friend has turned into a zombie even though she looks and sounds the same as ever. These and numerous others seem to defy embodiment, and yet when they are fully embraced physically and vocally, they are able to transport us into an imaginative space that can be dramatic and magical.

Most of us, when telling dreams, tend to think of them as a kind of movie in our head or a rapid series of slides. But if we intend to recreate and re-experience them, we have to make them three-dimensional. And it's not always obvious how to do this. How do you swim underwater, walk through a field of dismembered body parts, put an axe through the head of your baby brother, or make love to Catherine Zeta-Jones or Johnny Depp? You have to approach this work as an explorer, trying many different ways to stylize

---

4.   Greta had this dream at a time when she and her fiancé were having difficulties and she thought, perhaps, they should break up.

your images before you hit on the right thing. Treat each image like a foreign country and discover how you can best express its unique character.

Warming up without words

The goal in solo Dream Enactment is to recreate the dreamscape by narrating the dream while fully embodying all the images. This requires the dreamer to use her body and voice, not just her words, to convey the dream experience. Through sound and movement, she tries to suggest not only the facts of the dream but the emotional "flavor" of everything that happens. And not just what happens from the point of view of the dreamer: her body and voice should find a way to capture all the environments, all the characters, all the objects, all the actions from every point of view.

This takes practice, persistence, and creativity. Even experienced actors can find it challenging to tell a story while, at the same time, conveying the feeling tone of each moment. Anyone can accomplish this, though, by going image by image; that is, taking each important part of the story—in our case, the dream story—and finding a vocal and physical expression for what is happening. Actors sometimes call this "dropping in," that is, "dropping in" to the feeling tone of the moment using just your body and your voice.

You don't need to be an actor, though, to "drop in." Your imagination can lead you there if you just give yourself permission to express your dream, image by image, in sound and movement. To help make this feel more natural, I have suggested below some warm-ups that will help connect the physical and vocal exploration of dream images with the words that tell the story.

But before even warming up to this, you can try it on for size, if you like. Just think of the most important images in your dream, and see if you can find, for each key image, a sound and a movement that drops you into it. Experience the shape and the feeling tone of flying through the air, or fleeing from a psycho killer, or dancing with your dream lover using just sound and movement. In a group, it is a good idea for everyone to try this out simultaneously, with no one watching, so that you don't feel self-conscious about rolling around on the floor making weird noises, or jumping up and down laughing with glee.

The Sound/Motion Circle—a warm-up

A simple and effective warm-up to use to prepare you for telling dreams non-verbally is a Sound/Motion Circle. This group warm-up is simple enough for anyone to do it; at the same time, it is sufficiently engaging and challenging to hold the interest of experienced actors.

In this exercise, everyone in your group stands in a circle. Someone moves into the center of the circle and demonstrates a vocal sound with a physical action. Everyone in the circle then tries to imitate this.

The person in the center of the circle—let's call him the "conductor" — could be twirling, slithering, skipping, collapsing, or doing any other strong movement accompanied by an open vocal sound: *ahhh, oooh, ooof,* or *wheeeee!* He could be stomping like a giant, or rushing like a waterfall, or flapping like a bird. The sound should be responsive to the rhythm and quality of the movement. The sound and motion should be repeated over and over so that its form becomes clear to everyone in the group. Each member of the group tries to imitate the sound and motion as precisely as possible, not just the outer form but also the feeling it conveys. The conductor in the middle should go around the circle and look each person in the eye trying to convey the essence of the feeling behind the sound and movement. When he has gone at least once around the circle, he should choose someone who seems to have gotten the essence of his action to start a new sound and motion. He chooses this person simply by locking eyes with her and changing places with her, leaving her now in the center of the circle.

The new sound and motion should start where the last one left off. The new conductor should transform the earlier action into a new sound and motion by playing with it, improvising, making it faster, slower, clunkier, or more elegant, until it turns into something entirely different. If you are the new person in the center, try to make the transformation on the basis of how you are feeling in the moment; if you are tired or excited or anxious or angry, try to make a sound and motion that reflects that impulse. If everyone follows an inner impulse, a wide variety of movements and sounds will be sampled in a short time and the group should be energized and stimulated. When everyone has gone at least once, the warm-up can come to an end.

The Sound/Motion Dream Image (without words)

This variation on the Sound/Motion Circle not only warms people up, it also helps to put them in the atmosphere of dreams. It's a way of introducing a group to the wide range of feelings evoked by dreams, opening a window into the personal connection each person has with his or her own dream.

In this exercise, instead of going into the center of the circle with an abstract sound and motion, the conductor enters the circle with a sound and a motion that embodies a particular dream image. It's helpful if he chooses an image that's central to the dream, one that carries the most emotional weight. He could be flying above his childhood home, picking up a dead goldfish, opening a door into a scary room. Or he could be his mother waving up at him, or the dead goldfish itself, or the scary thing that hides behind the door. Whatever the image, the conductor should use an open sound and clear movement to convey that particular dream moment. If there is no sound associated with the image—a dead goldfish, after all, makes no sound—the conductor should make a sound that goes to the *feeling* of the image. What does it feel like to be the dead goldfish? Again, the members of the group should imitate this sound and motion not just for its outer form, but for the emotional quality that underlies it. It should seem as if the conductor's sound/motion image is being reflected in the multiple mirrors of the group.

As a variation on this, some people might want to portray, as a central image, contrasting moments in the dream—for instance, reaching nervously into a dark sewer and finding the cutest, softest kitten; or laboriously climbing up the tallest mountain and then joyfully jumping off into an abyss. These images would be conveyed non-verbally, but with contrasting sounds and motions. While there should be no hard-and-fast rule for how many different sounds and motions can be used, the group should try to stick to simple, repetitive actions and not try to tell more than a single, central image in the dream—or, at most, two closely related contrasting images.

Most people will want to take a moment to prepare an image from a particular dream because it is not always obvious which image is most essential or how to stylize the image through a repetitive sound and movement. For inexperienced groups, it might be helpful to introduce this warm-up using childhood dreams, which tend to be already distilled in memory into a few vivid images. Experienced groups find it more challenging to use images from very recent dreams, because these tend to contain more surprises.

The Sound/Motion Dream Image (with words)

This is the same warm-up as before—creating a Sound/Motion Image—only this time, the repetitive sound and movement is accompanied by a phrase or two that identifies or describes the image. The dreamer first repeats the action and vocal expression (but without words) three or four times until the entire group can follow along with sound and movement. Then he "floats" words on "top" of the physical action and vocal expression while the rest of the group tries to imitate him. In other words, he lets the language emerge out of the sound and movement, using the language to identify or describe the image.

Some identifying phrases could be:

"I'm gonna get you, little boy! I'm gonna get you!"

"I'm losing my teeth. Oh my, god. I'm losing my teeth!"

"Higher, higher, higher . . . Jump! Higher, higher, higher . . . Jump!"

Some descriptive, narrative phrases could be:

"The cold, dark sun at The End of the World."

"Oh, what a beautiful gown. What a beautiful wedding gown!"

"The Zombie King keeps coming and coming and coming."

Or you could float language over sounds and motions that *both* identify and describe an image:

"Get it off! Get it off! The cat keeps scratching me! Get it off!"

Whatever language you use, have it come directly out of the vocal and physical action, and be emblematic of that image. This is an essential exercise to prepare for solo Dream Enactment: floating words on top of sound/motion images. We will talk about this more in Part Two; for now it is enough to say that when you narrate the whole dream, your goal is to constantly transform your body and voice to allow the language to embody each and every image. In other words, the language is given its rhythms, its tones, its sensuality, by following the actions of the body and voice.

In the early stages of doing this warm-up, the sound and motion that captures the essence of a dream image may seem like a caricature, or at least a very broad stroke. This is not necessarily a bad thing. It gives the group a clear direction for the dream, which the enactment process will refine. Also, in the beginning, it will seem awkward for some people to be describing an image while embodying it. That is, it may feel strange to be inside the image and outside at the same time. It takes practice to master this.

These warm-ups using a single, central dream image model the progression to be used for exploring how to re-enact the whole dream. First, you will show the dream without words, dropping into all the images; then, you will tell the dream with words floating the language on top of the fully embodied images.

Playing All the Parts

Presenting the dream without words

Having warmed up as a group with the Sound/Motion Circles, exploring individual images with and without words, you're ready for the next step: telling the whole dream with and without words. We'll start, as we started in the warm-ups, without words.

Here you select a partner to whom you will show the entire dream non-verbally, relying only on sound and movement to convey the images. It usually works best for the whole group to split up into pairs who work separately at this process until everyone is ready to present to the whole group.

To the extent it is possible non-verbally, try to explore *all* the details: all the scenes, characters, objects, and actions. Remember, while it's important to try to follow the story of the dream in sound and movement, it's even more important to drop into the feeling tone of each moment. Later, when language is included in the enactment of the dream, it will be essential for you to go back to this feeling tone to drop into the emotional heart of the dream.

The first time doing this, most people tend to rush through the dream. It seems hard to tell the details and nuances of the dream without using words. This becomes easier, though, if you let go of the notion that your partner has to understand everything that you do, and focus instead on making your partner *feel* each moment.

Try to find the essence of each detail. Take your time. This exercise is primarily an opportunity for you to explore your dream and only secondarily for your partner to receive it. To the extent that you, as a dream explorer now, can slow it down and take your time, the richer your experience will be. Don't just show the images in general; try to find the details in the settings, the changes in the characters, the various feeling tones of the objects, and the various reactions to the actions in the dream.

If you are dreaming that it's your wedding day and you are wearing a beautiful, elegant wedding dress, but are very anxious because you don't know who the groom is, you need to find, somehow, without words, both the beauty of the dress and your nervousness inside of it.

Because no words are used, it may be helpful for the dreamer to act as if her partner comes from another country (or from another planet) and doesn't speak her language. The partner will act as a scribe. The scribe's role is to watch and take notes, to be a fair witness, recording all the physical actions, noticing all the different sounds, and writing them down. Even if the scribe doesn't understand everything that is happening, he tries to catch the shape of all the images and catch the feeling tone.

For the dream about the bride in the beautiful wedding dress who is so anxious because she doesn't know who the groom is, the scribe might write down:

Elegant walk

Singing, happy

Smells flowers

Looks at ring
Nervous hands
Wild eyes
Looking around, frantic
Whimpering; something's wrong

The purpose of this image list is actually as much to train the eye of the scribe as it is to offer helpful feedback to the dreamer. The scribe needs to see that the images exist not in the words but in the actions of body and voice. This will be particularly important to guard against a disembodied recitation of the dream story, or to clarify which images are being enacted if the dreamer decides to overlap more than one, creating a kind of double exposure. It is good, then, from the very beginning to see the full range of vocal and physical imagery undistracted by the specificity of words.

The hardest thing to do in this or *any* presentation of the dream is to remember to view the dream from every perspective. The temptation is always to tell the dream solely from your own perspective—from the point of view of the "I" narrator. We will talk about this more when we discuss the telling of the dream in words; but for now it is enough to say that you have to play all the parts of the dream, not just yourself. If you meet the President in your dream, you have to be the President as well as yourself, and probably the secret service men, too.

This can be challenging: how do you find a sound and a motion that can convey what it is like for the President to meet you? What sound and motion can capture the inner life of those secret service men?

It is important in this exploration to make an *open* sound with every image—ahhh, oooh, oooo—not a whisper or a whistle or a clicking; that is, use a vocal tone that can carry language. This is preparation for telling the dreams verbally when you will float language on top of the sound and movement. So each image must have its voice. This is true even if there is no sound in the dream. The sounds you make are not necessarily what is *heard* in the dream, but the feeling that is evoked by the image. Walking through a silent, scary woods may evoke frightened cries or whimpers. Flying through the sky into outer space evokes exhilarating calls of wonder. The mountain that is impossible to climb might give a low rumble of obstinate power.

In this stage of the work, you are trying to get to the essence of an image through movement and sound. So don't feel that you have to be too literal about what is happening. If you are fishing by a peaceful pond on a glorious sunny day, it is more important to convey how peaceful, glorious, and sunny it is than to show, like in the game of charades, how you cast out your line to catch fish. Similarly, if you have an angry phone conversation with your dad in your dream, it's more important that you show the different feelings expressed on both sides than to talk gibberish into your hand to convey "talking on the phone." The explanation of the images will become clear once we use words; but for now, try to distill the moments into vivid vocal and physical packages.

Finally, it is sometimes helpful, even at this stage, to set up the geography of the dream. If in your dream you walk up a mountain, find someplace in the room to climb up. If you are in a cave or a closet in your dream, perhaps nestle into the corner of the room to get the feeling of a tight space. The effect of placing yourself in a physical space similar to your dreamscape will make the dream come alive for you and might even help you remember long lost details.

Presenting the dream with words

Before you enact the dream with the help of words, it is important to understand the notion of floating language on top of sound and movement. We do this naturally in real life when we're very passionate about something: our words take on the coloring of our tone of voice, and our body language. Everyone can do it. People who don't consider themselves actors at all find this very helpful in embodying images. This technique helps you "act" like an actor, even if you have no theater training.

If you are using a raspy voice and jerky movements to describe a killer breaking down your front door, your words should be raspy and jerky. If you are using a breathy voice and graceful movements to describe flying through the clouds, your words should be breathy and graceful. In other words, if a person from a foreign country were to hear this language, he would understand its feeling quality by tone and action even if the literal meaning escapes him.

This is similar to the storytelling techniques you would use telling a dream around the campfire, but more exacting. The enactor is required to eliminate the neutral narrator altogether and to *only* tell the dream from inside one image or another. This means that, while speaking, he is constantly changing body and voice to suit the changing imagery. But the trick is: he is always *telling* the story, maintaining a narrative element. It is as if the story of the dream is always being told through the filter of one image or another.

Let's take a childhood dream of mine, and imagine how we might float language on top of the narrative.

The Cackling Witch Dream

I had a repeating dream as a kid, and, in this dream, I am always walking through a dark scary woods. There are patches of snow on the ground and birch trees all around with patches of white and brown bark looming over me.

Suddenly, the ground opens up and—*ohhhh!*—I'm sliding down a curving slide *aiiiiieeee*. I hear a voice below cackling—heh heh heh heh heh. It's the Witch from Snow White! I'm gonna get you! I'm gonna get you! Heh heh heh.

Aiiiiiieeee at the bottom of the slide I catch a glimpse of her cauldron and—*ahhhh!* That wakes me up.

Floating language on top of imagery might start even with the opening phrase, "I had a repeating dream as a kid . . ." It should already sound dark and scary, as if the fact of the dream repeating is dark and scary like the woods.

There are patches of snow on the ground and birch trees all around with patches of white and brown bark looming over me.

Here, the patchiness of white and brown should be expressed in gesture, and maybe even a textured, "patchy" voice, and, of course, something in your body and voice should be "looming."

Suddenly, the ground opens up and—ohhhh!—I'm sliding down a curving slide aiiiiieeeeeeee!

Falling movement and a sliding voice could evoke this image.

I hear a voice below cackling—heh heh heh heh heh.

Here the dreamer might transform from a sliding body and voice into a wicked witch body and voice.

It's the Witch from Snow White!

This too could be said in the Witch's voice, even though the information is *about* the witch.

"I'm gonna get you. I'm gonna get you! Heh heh heh."

Even though the Witch never said anything, this is sort of what she was thinking—an evil, teasing kind of thought.

Aiiiiiieeee at the bottom of the slide I catch a glimpse of her cauldron and—ahhhh! That wakes me up.

The dreamer transforms back to the sliding, falling, terrified voice and narrates the ending—*ahhh! That wakes me up!*—with the same trembling surprise that occurred at the time of waking from the dream.

The challenge in this dream, as in so many dreams, is to make the woods and the witch, *really* mean and scary—not funny or childish—and to make my own fright real and not phony or forced. This takes practice, which is what our rehearsal process is all about: exploring the images to capture all the details and to plumb their emotional depths.

Embodying all the images

The first run-through of the dream using words is meant to follow fast on the heels of the non-verbal telling of the dream, and imitates it as much as possible. The dreamer should try to tell the dream in the same way as before, using sound and movement to get to the essence of each dream image. The only difference is, in this version, you can use words to describe the dream, floating the narrative on top of your ever-changing vocal sounds and body movements.

During this run-through—the first telling of the dream in words—it's important to commit to the embodiment of *all* the images: all the settings, all the characters, all the objects, all the actions. Even the style of the dream should be considered an image. Don't worry, though, about getting the "right" words. It's much more important that you drop deeply into the images and let language flow from the re-experience of your dream.

Tell the dream verbally to the same partner you worked with before, immediately after you tell them the dream without using words. This way you can vividly remember the vocal and physical work you used for each image originally, and can float the narrative over those sounds and movements. Your partner will again act as scribe, writing down everything you say and do.

At this stage, it is easy to fall back into the common habit of telling the dream only from the image of yourself. At all cost, avoid the temptation to tell the entire dream from your own perspective—from the point of view of the "I" narrator. A good rule of thumb is that, at least half the time, you will tell the dream from inside the image of someone or something other than yourself. *The trees are looming over me . . .* is to be told with the body and voice of the looming trees, not my small, scared self. *As I fall I hear a witch cackling . . .* is to be told with the body and voice of the cackling witch, not with the voice of the fall or the fear.

Some contemporary dream work is based on the idea that *all* the characters in a dream are aspects or reflections of ourselves. Even if this is partly true—they are surely aspects of our imaginations—by calling them reflections of ourselves we run the risk of making the dream ego-centric, all about the "I" narrator. So I am not suggesting that you go all the way and actually, as narrator, assume the identity of the characters or settings, saying, *"I am the witch . . ."* or *"I am the looming trees."* The witch is the witch and the trees are the trees. If you know what is in their minds, by all means say so: *"I'm gonna get you!"* But don't go so far as to make *them* the "I" narrator. Reserve the narrative voice for yourself in the dream and use the third person for everyone else. Otherwise, the characterizations can get confusing and misleading.

To help keep the balance between the "I" narrator and all the other perspectives, put particular focus on the following categories of images that need to be given their own point of view: settings, characters, objects, actions.

Dream settings: Dreamscapes—the landscapes of the dream—are essential images that define, contain, and often influence the other dream images. *"I'm in an airport," "I'm in my garden," "I'm in a castle under the sea."* The body and voice you give to these places need to describe not only their architecture, but their qualities. Is the airport vast or busy or empty? Is the garden fruitful or dying or weed-infested? Is the castle a place of safety or danger or nobility? There are many more questions we could ask of these dreamscapes but at the very least the essential qualities need to be embodied.

Dream settings also include all the environments and atmospheres in the dream: the temperature of the water, the golden light of the sun, the ugliness of the oppressive, gray walls. You might also include in this category the elegance of a tuxedo, or the enticing smell of a pizza. And, of course, feelings, sensations, and emotions of every variety are part of the dream environment: the trashy, sexy feeling of a honky-tonk bar; the impressive competence of the mechanics busily working on your car; the frightening, unnatural quiet in the deserted street outside your childhood home. All these must be given physicality and a vocal quality as you describe them. They may be connected with how you yourself are feeling in the dream, but often there will be a significant difference between the environment itself and how you feel in that environment.

For example, the tuxedo may be elegant, but you are feeling insecure. The bar may be trashy and sexy, but you are feeling uptight and puritanical. The mechanics are working most efficiently, but you are impatient. Your home is eerily quiet, but you want to scream. The walls at work are oppressive and gray, but you are going about your business as usual seemingly unaffected by their ugliness.

While the settings may affect how you're feeling in the dream, give

them an independent place in your image score and allow them to resonate on their own terms. You might want to return to the image of the
dream settings a number of times to enable them to act as containers for
the feeling tone of the dream.

Dream characters: It's pretty obvious on the surface how to embody dream
characters—take on a different body and voice for each character, both
when you are describing them and when they are talking or thinking. What
isn't so obvious is the possibility of telling parts of the dream through their
eyes. Sometimes telling what happens to *you* in the dream can be much
more powerful from their point of view.

> *I had a dream and in this dream there is a bull elephant trumpeting
> and pacing up and down, and I am afraid he is going to attack me.*

The beginning of this dream could be told from the point of view of
the fear, dropping into elephant voice only to describe the creature "pac-
ing up and down." But it is much more affecting, I think, to tell it in the
hulking body and husky voice of the elephant, even the part about how
"I was afraid he was going to attack me." A little fear might creep into the
elephant's voice as if the image of my fear was superimposed on the image
of the elephant, but the audience will understand by the words that it is
my fear and not the elephant's. Even more challenging would be to switch
places and see yourself through the eyes of the elephant:

> *The elephant keeps pacing and trumpeting, irritated that I am so scared.
> He wants me to climb on his back, but I don't know that. I am blinded
> by my fear.*

By "characters" in dreams I mean any person, creature, or thing that
has consciousness or intention: the clock on the wall with a human face;
the white buck that wants you to follow it; even the mountain that's out
to kill you. By entering into the intentions of the different characters, you
can sometimes learn more about yourself in the dream.

Often the hardest character to embody is yourself. When I say, "I am afraid the elephant is going to attack me," I am assuming the audience knows who I am. But this is not the case. Not only are you different ages in dreams, but you are often expressing different aspects of yourself. Finding different bodies and voices for the character called "Me" and "I" is frequently the hardest thing to do.

Dream objects: Not all objects in dreams need to be embodied physically. If you are in your bathroom, you don't have to "be" a toilet, a sink, or a bathtub, unless there's something special about them. And even if there is something special, you can often get your point across by substituting a chair for the toilet, a night table for the sink, and a big cardboard box for the bathtub. In other words, if you are sitting at your kitchen table and a golden light is shining through the window, you might want to simply focus on the golden light and let a table be the table. Certainly you don't have to "be a table" just because there is a table in the dream.

Some objects, though, are so special, so redolent with meaning or emotion, that they deserve to be fully explored with body and voice. The sound of the witch's cauldron, for instance, might be worth investigating; likewise, the magic of the tiny shell in The Dream of the Shell & the Storm.

Often, if the object is small enough—a hat, a knife, a pill—you will have the choice of becoming the object or using the object. If you choose to become the object, it's usually better to embody its qualities rather than its physical proportions. The grandeur of the hat, the precision of the knife, and the tranquilizing effect of the pill are essential; the words you use to describe the object can give us the actual picture of it.

Occasionally, if the object in your dream exists in real life, it might be good to bring in the thing itself. Your prom dress might still exist; likewise your father's old typewriter. If you were eating a banana in your dream, why not bring in a banana? If you wore your favorite bandana in a dream, why not wear it?

Dream actions: Because we're telling dreams from the perspective of all the images, dream actions can be tricky. In a dream of cutting off the head of a dragon, there are two actions, not just one. From your point of view, the key action is slaying the dragon: the sword cutting through the neck. From the dragon's point of view, the key action is being slain: its head flying off the sword. Almost all actions that are interactions between you and another character or object have more than one point of view.

Another problem with dream actions is that they are often difficult to portray because they are frequently on a scale that is either larger or smaller than human size, or not human at all, such as the actions of a monster or an ant. Since you only have your own body and voice to enact these images you have to stylize the actions, using your body and voice to capture some part or some essence of the action. Flying through a wall, wild sex in an elevator, or the explosion of an atomic bomb need to be suggested by a rhythm, a gesture, or a sound to allow us to imagine their full affect. Otherwise, the images are in danger of becoming trivial or funny.

Dream styles: Some dreams seem to come in a recognizable style. Sometimes you are even aware of the style in the dream. One dream feels like a superhero movie. Another seems like a teenage romance. A third is set in a medieval landscape. If this is the case, you might make this style part of the presentation. Don't force it, but don't avoid it.

> *It is like a James Bond movie.*
>
> *Everything is in brilliant technicolor.*
>
> *I feel like any minute I will hear jungle drums.*

Even when the dream doesn't fall into a particular genre, the style of the dream (or at least the style in which it is remembered) is an important component in helping your audience receive your dream. If part of your dream is very confusing in memory, tell that part in a confused manner. If a character seems to resemble not one but two or more people in your real life, tell about each one of them. If you see a crowd but only remember one face and every other person is a vague blur, don't make up details or associations about the indistinct personages; let the vagueness be a quality of the image and tell it like it is. If the dream is a repetitive dream, one you have dreamt over and over again, you might even want to tell it more than once.

Suddenly the scene shifts.

I forget what happens after that but the next thing I know . . .

I kept dreaming this dream all night in variations . . .

I woke up so confused.

These are typical "style" remarks that could be included in your first telling of the dream.

Dream voice: It is good practice to tell the dream in the present tense as a reminder that, when you are dreaming, you *are* in the present. The present tense also supports a sense of discovery and surprise when something unexpected happens in the dream. In fact, it's a good idea to tell the dream as if you don't know how it will develop or end. This is hard to do when you first tell the dream; but, paradoxically, with rehearsal it becomes easier to act as if you've never told the dream before.

But, since dreams are always a kind of negotiation between the images as you experienced them and the images as you remember them now, and since this exercise is an enactment of past dreams, telling the dream in the past tense is fine, too. Some people feel more comfortable storytelling in this manner, and, as long as they act as if everything is happening to them in the moment, the dream can be experienced with as much immediacy if told in the past tense.

The narrative thread

Maintaining a narrative thread out to your audience while dropping into the imagery is like rubbing your stomach and patting your head at the same time. The more you speak out to your listeners, the more you tend to drop out of the images, and the more you drop into the images, the more you tend to forget about who you are talking to. The art of this work is to do both in equal measure.

Notice in my childhood Witch Dream (see p. 60) how the script goes back and forth between a descriptive narrative—"*I am walking through a dark scary woods*"—an immediate, emotional narrative—"*ohhhh! I'm sliding down*

a curving slide aiiiiieeee"—and a narrative from the Witch's point of view—
"I'm gonna get you! Heh heh heh." Switching the narrative focus requires the
dreamer to stay inside the dream material to re-experience it, while, at the
same time, communicating what happened so that the audience can experience it too.

This practice of simultaneously being inside and outside the work can
be profound. It goes to the core of the art of acting that requires performers
to be present in the moment while aware of the artifice they are creating. It
goes to the core of dream work in that it uncovers both the specific and the
universal quality of the imagery. It goes to the core of Dream Enactment in
that it reminds us to explore our personal experience not just for our own
sake, but for the sake of others: our audience, our listeners, our fellow dreamers. Ultimately, it can become a core practice of self-discovery as we attempt
to remain aware of ourselves moment by moment while watching ourselves
from afar go through our life's dance.

Banishing the neutral narrator

The consequence of telling the dream from inside all the images is that you
are never a neutral bystander. Everything is an image and you are always
inside the dream. There is no place for a neutral narrator, the voice that, like
some objective newscaster, simply reports the facts of the dream or the notes
scribbled in your dream notebook. You are always coloring your voice with
the feeling tone of the image and finding movement that expresses the action
of any given moment in the dream.

Even background information that is needed to understand what's going
on should find an evocative expression, by floating the information over an
accompanying image—that is, saying the information in the voice and physicality of the image.

*I am in Chicago in the warehouse district. I have never been to Chicago
in real life, but in this dream I am in Chicago and it looks like a picture
I once saw of London during the Blitz.*

A body and voice that look and feel like bombed-out rubble ought to accompany this information so that the fact of the Chicago warehouse district can be part of the London Blitz feeling tone.

Occasionally you may come across a dream character who seems unemotional, or a setting that seems "normal" and unremarkable. See if you can find the coldness or remoteness in that lack of emotion, or the comfort and familiarity in the normal setting. What seems neutral may in fact have subtle feelings associated with it. Try to find them.

The radio version

One way to banish the neutral narrator and explore the sensuality of all the images is to practice a "radio" version of your dream. In this exercise, you ask your partner to close her eyes, and then you tell the dream as if you were performing it on the radio, a dramatic radio program, maybe even with sound effects.

Instantly, it will become clear that the only way to convey the texture of the dream is by coloring your voice to fit each image, by transforming it for each character, setting, object, and action. Your grandfather has to have an old man's voice; the tornado outside has to have a stormy, tempestuous sound; the hot soup on the stove has to have a yummy, hearty feel to it; the race you are running has to sound exhilarating and exhausting. By transforming your voice through pitch, rhythm, tone, and articulation, you can follow the image score of your dream. Your partner can give you feedback as to which images, if any, were simply reported neutrally and which seemed sensuous and alive to the imagination. Then, having practiced your score using voice alone, you can add more easily the movements and gestures that can accompany the transformations.

Color work: a "floating words" exercise

The hardest thing to master for all dreamers, whether they have acting training or not, is the full embodiment of language. It is not just a question of skill: allowing your body and your voice to reflect precisely what you are saying requires a full commitment to the image. When you say "hot," your voice should sound hot; when you say "sad" your body should reflect your sorrow; when you say, as Juliet does, "Gallop apace, you fiery-footed steeds," you should put a galloping, fiery energy in your rhythm, your tone, your posture, your gestures.

There are exceptions to this guideline, most notably when your body or voice reflects just the opposite of what you're saying in order to convey how difficult it is for you to say it. For instance, when someone says "I don't love you," but they *do* love you and are finding it hard to admit it. The point, though, is that it is essential to try to make physical and vocal choices that reflect the content of the language.

To practice the skill of using embodied language, you might try an exercise in "color" work. In this work, you create three very different characters: a "Red" character, a "Blue" character, and a "Yellow" character. "Red" might be blood red, or rusty red; "Yellow" might be sunshine yellow, or puke yellow; "Blue" might be Caribbean blue, or midnight blue. Out of these images, you can create a character (or rather a caricature) of a person with a distinct "Red," "Yellow," or "Blue" body movement, rhythm, and tone of voice. To practice how they speak in their "color," have them say the pledge of allegiance or some neutral text like a newspaper article. Two or more of you could even take turns as partners interviewing the Color characters, asking them what they do for a living, what their favorite movie is, or whether they have a boyfriend or girl-friend. Whatever you do, keep them talking in their red, yellow, or blue tone of voice, using their red, yellow, or blue rhythms and movements.

If you have time, and interest in acting exercises, you might then go to a monologue from a play, and create a "color score" that would be appropriate for the character, this time using the real "colors" or qualities of the character. If you were playing Hamlet, for instance, you might create vocal rhythms, tones, and body movements that reflect Hamlet's blue-black melancholy, his day-glow yellow fake madness, and his blood-red thirst for revenge. Score these "colors" to any of Hamlet's monologues and you can practice floating language (in this case, Shakespeare's text) over Hamlet's mood swings, fol-lowing his erratic and conflicting behavior.

Finally, you might take your dream and create a "color" for each of the major images in the dream. This would create a "color score," a palette of movement, rhythm, and tone, to illuminate your language. For instance, in my Cackling Witch Dream, the witch's text would be black, of course; the dark woods, a somber dark green; my cry of fear, perhaps, an ugly orange; and the bubbling cauldron, a vomit yellow. By attaching colors to the text, you might be able to see more clearly how the language of the dream "floats" over the vocal and physical behavior you attach to each colored image.

The role of the scribe

While you are rolling around on the floor, or jumping up on tables, enacting your dream without words, your partner should be writing down a list of what you do and what you sound like. Perhaps she will put a check mark next to any sounds or movements that seem particularly evocative. At the end, she will hand you a list of images which will help you remember what you did.

Practically, though, the scribe in this first round of telling is mainly there to act as an audience so that you never forget that you are trying to tell your dream *to* someone, not simply exploring it for your own enjoyment. The scribe is also trying to train her eye to become more sensitive to how the body and voice of an actor create imagery. By following the form of the images rather than their content, the scribe can get a better idea of how to create her own imagery. By noticing which images move her most, she may also get some creative ideas about how to stylize the most moving moments of her own dream.

When you start to tell the dream with words, the scribe's role becomes more demanding. To keep track of your imagery, your partner will help you create an "image score," the series of images expressed through sound, movement, and words that makes up your dream narrative. This is similar to a musical score, only made up of images rather than notes.

Suddenly, I find myself in a vast, dry, windy desert.

The scribe will not just write down "desert," but "vast," "dry," "windy" as well: three different nuances of the image that you will want to embody physically or vocally. The scribe will also write down, as accurately as possible, what you do physically and vocally.

Scanning horizon. Raspy voice.

The image score will be your road map as you tell the dream more and more. At first, it will be a template on which you will add new images as you discover them. In telling a dream for the first time, you will inevitably leave out some details, and the scribe will help you fill in the gaps. Later, the completed image score will help you remember the intricacies of the dream since, after rehearsing the dream many times, you may begin to drop out some of the details because you think they are obvious.

The scribe and the dreamer work together to build a road map for the dream presentation. Every time the dream is told, the scribe should keep a record of what is said and done so that more and more details can be added. Often, so much will be going on that the scribe cannot possibly record it all; that's okay—there's always another rehearsal to fill in the gaps.

The initial exploration

These first enactments of your dream, with words and without, are the foundation for your later work. It is important to give enough time for exploration. You are beginning to change your relationship to the dream from one that is strictly in your imagination to one that is physically present in the room. You are looking for physical, vocal, and verbal choices that make you feel like you are deeply inside the fabric of the dream. Allow yourself to search for the choices that resonate most accurately with your first experience of the dream.

To begin, find a space that in some way resembles the topography of your dream. Give yourself a physical analogy, if you can, to the dreamscape you remember using a doorway or window, a staircase or corner wall, a platform or the middle of the floor.

Then you and your partner will each enact a dream first without words and then with words, while the other acts as scribe. Avoid the temptation to talk about the dream after you tell it; but rather take a moment to reflect on what parts of the dream you slid over, avoided, or forgot, and make a mental note to explore those more fully the next time around.

Solo Dream Showings

Informal presentations

After practicing the dream with a partner—perhaps getting feedback, and rehearsing it a few times—you might want to present the dream to a larger group, perhaps even create an informal dream show. To help fill out your narrative, you and your partner can look at the "Dream Q & A" section in Part Two for some ideas on how to ask each other leading questions about your dreams. Even without reading those sections, though, natural empathy should lead you to the same goal of discovering the depths and nuances of your dreams by asking one another common sense questions: *"What did the whale look like?" "How did it feel to ride its tail?"*

Together, you might also decide where to perform your dreams, considering places in the room that best evoke the spatial relationships of the dream. It you were on top of a mountain in a dream, stand on a table. If you were in a cave in a dream, squat under a table. In creating an informal dream show, it is helpful to move the audience around in order to keep changing the perspective on the dream landscapes.

There are also suggestions in Part Two about making your dream even more evocative by using a special prop, or a vivid costume piece, or even a little lighting effect such as a candle. You might even want to give your dream a title to underscore the central image or action of the dream. These theatrical frills, however, are much less important than the depth of feeling you display and the honesty with which you approach the experience of the dream.

Informal presentations should remain just that: low key. There should be no room for a lot of performance anxiety. Either perform for your own group or invite only the kind of friends or colleagues you feel will be supportive. And to minimize the stress and maximize the fun, your major acting challenge should be only to be yourself: speaking in your own voice, acknowledging the audience, and telling the story as if around a campfire.

The Image Check-in: a performance warm-up

Before rehearsal or performance, an easy and efficient way to get everyone in the group into a dream space and out of the bustle of daily life is an Image Check-in. Standing in a tight circle, shoulder to shoulder, eyes closed, everyone thinks about the dream images they have been preparing. Then, in no particular order, with no particular leader, people call out images that they recall from their dream or from some other dream that they have heard: a character, a setting, an object, an action. Everyone in the group repeats the image three or four times until someone else interrupts with a new image:

Ahhh, warm, green water. Ahhh, warm, green water.

Omigod we're gonna die. Omigod we're gonna die.

The blind man knows. The blind man knows.

This choral, verbal warm-up is so easy that any group can do it. It is especially helpful if the group is weary of rehearsals, or just exhausted from the grind of the day and needs a transition into physical work. Often you can slide naturally from the Image Check-in to a more physical Sound/Motion Circle just by stepping back, opening your eyes, and putting a little body action into the images you call out.

Framing the dream story

Because dreams are so enigmatic, it is helpful to your audience to know when the dream begins and ends. I like to introduce each presentation by saying "I had a dream, and in this dream . . ." (or words to that effect), and to end each presentation with "And that was the end of my dream" (or words to that effect). Even here, though, banish the neutral narrator and say these introductory and concluding phrases in the body and voice of the first and last images, keeping the imagery resonating even in the most prosaic phrases.

Finally, it is important to end each performance with applause. This is not a gesture to make the actors feel how great they were, or how entertaining their dreams were, but rather an acknowledgement, an appreciation, for the work that was done. Applause is the traditional framing device that ends the work for both performer and audience.

Enacting your partner's dreams

A more intricate exercise for exploring dreams in a group is a presentation in which dreamers do not present their own dreams but their partner's dreams. This can be a profound experience for both the dreamer and the partner. It takes a lot of empathy to enter deeply and accurately into someone else's dream. It is also very moving and illuminating, at times, to view your dream from an outside, objective perspective. This approach is particularly valuable for groups of people who are trying to get to know one another on a more personal level: a group made up of people from different backgrounds, nationalities, occupations, or simply a new group that is about to embark on an intense project or program. It takes a good deal of coaching on the part of each partner, but is good practice for learning how to enter the psychic landscape of another. Again, sections in Part Two give suggestions about how to coach someone to play the different images and actions in your dream. However, the rule of thumb is: don't *tell* your partner what to do, *show* your partner what to do.

Rediscovering your dream

Despite the informality of these dream presentations, there is one performance goal that everyone should try to accomplish: the rediscovery of the dream. After telling the dream a number of times, making an image score, perhaps answering questions about the details of the dream, the narrator naturally starts to think of the dream as a thing of the past, like a trip to the Grand Canyon. To be true to the dream in performance, even in an informal performance, the narrator has to encounter the dream again as if she doesn't know what's going to happen next. Assume that the dream is unfolding before you. This is as much a state of mind as it is an acting technique. Don't just embody the images, encounter them, react to them. Try to tell the dream as if it's all happening for the first time.

Naturally, if something in the dream surprised you, act surprised. But even in those moments that aren't overtly surprising, try to perform the dream as if you're experiencing it in the present rather than as a memory. In this spirit, be prepared to discover new things—and to act upon them—even in the midst of performing it.

A Sample Solo Script

Here is an example of a solo dream presentation, fully scripted: Teddy's Egg Creature Dream.[5] It should give you a sense of how someone might transform from image to image and still follow a narrative story step-by-step. Imagine Teddy's voice and body changing with each major image. The dream is written out as if there were many characters because, indeed, it has to be presented with many voices, which reflect the changing imagery.

For instance, the first voice is "Teddy's Pennsylvania Voice" reflecting Teddy's feeling that Pennsylvania is Nowhere-land. When Teddy speaks in his own voice, it's the voice of a young man who has been raised to be one of the best and the brightest—his parents' Prince—but who has some impulses, which, perhaps, are not so wholesome. Unfortunately, not all the nuances of his transformations in performance—small images within larger images—can be conveyed in a script without it becoming too cumbersome and confusing. But I think you'll get the idea of how he changes voices and transforms physically to tell the story and embody the images. Keep in mind, the dreamer, Teddy, plays all the parts.

---

5. All scripted dreams in this book were developed through improvisations and conversations with the actors. They try to capture the informal, natural voice of the dreamer. However, most dreams should not be scripted at all, but should follow only an image score, with occasional set phrases and events when precise cues are needed. Only the dreams in Part Three: Making Dream Theater are meant to have set and precise wording, because they're part of more formal theater productions. Even these scripts, though, are meant to sound like they come from a personal, natural voice.

Teddy's Egg Creature Dream

Teddy's Pennsylvania Voice:

(Driving image)

I hate Pennsylvania. Pennsylvania really pisses me off. I've driven between Idaho and Boston a dozen times it seems, and every time I go through Pennsylvania it's foggy and rainy and lonely, and I can't find a goddam place to stop. The roads are awful, the people—if you can find 'em—are stupid and rude, and it just feels like nowhere.

So that's how I feel about Pennsylvania: it's nowhere.

Shack Voice:

(Clutter image)

So in this dream, I'm in a shack in the heart of PA, a shack built on top of a dirt mound, like you see at a construction site; a shack, in other words, in the middle of nowhere. And in the middle of this shack there's this little kitchenette-type area, with a counter and refrigerator and all like that. Hard to say what's there, 'cause it's really run down and cluttered. It's not a nice shack.

Everyday Voice:

(Discovering eggs)

Anyway, I decide to eat something. So I go to the refrigerator, and open it up and there's nothing in it . . . except eggs.

(He holds up a carton of a half-dozen eggs)

So I figure: "Okay, I'll have some eggs."

(He cracks an egg.)

I mean, I'm not really hungry but I decide to eat anyway. Like: I'm here, so I might as well eat. Why not?

(He cracks another egg)

Nothing else to . . .

(We hear a huge cracking sound)

Blue Flash Voice:

Suddenly: there's a blue flash in the pan, a blinding light, like a lightning bolt, and then . . . and then . . .

(He stares in awe)

Awe Voice:

This . . . this thing comes out of the eggs. It's just there all of a sudden—on the other side of the counter. This dome-shaped thing.

(He examines it in wonder. We hear the sound of a quiet Creature: mmmmmmm)

Slime Voice:

It's like about four feet, four and a half feet, tall. And it's . . . it's slimy. Kind of like when you . . . if you . . . if you boil eggs there's that . . . that white-blue egg-white stuff. That's what it's got all over the outside of it: egg slime.

Ripping Mouth Voice:

And . . . and it has a mouth. Its mouth is just this rip or something in the flesh. And it's . . . it looks like . . . you know, if you . . . if you imagine a gash in your stomach or something—how the skin would be if it was a really rough knife rip or something, and inside . . . Oh! It's pink. Yeah. It's really pink like . . . like bloody gums or something.

(Making the sound of the ripping Creature)

Creature:

Arrrrrrgggggghhhhh . . .

Ripping Mouth Voice:

It keeps coming in and out of the rip: just this pink little beak-type-teeth thing that comes in and out of the slime and chomps like mad.

(Demonstrating)

Creature:

Arrrrrgggggghhhhhh….

(He walks cautiously around it, deliberating)

Watchful Voice:

At first … at first I'm frightened because I don't know what it is and it's really gross and I don't know what it's going to do. But I watch … yeah, and wait, and … and eventually I realize that—yeah!—it isn't going to do anything at all to me.

Realization Voice:

That it's mine.

(He considers this)

Hmm … It's mine because I had been making the eggs. Sure! They were my eggs. Of course!

(We hear a low sound: the waiting Creature: mmmmm)

Questioning Voice:

So … ?

(Pause. Sound of the waiting Creature: mmmmm)

So … ?

(Demonstrating how the Creature waits: mmmmm)

Slime Voice:

It just stands there: Mmmmm. Sliming! Mmmmm. Sliming!

(Demonstrating the ripping mouth)

Creature:

Arrrrggggggghhhhhh! Arrrrrggggggghhhhhh!

It almost seems like it's standing there being disgusting for the sake of being disgusting.

Exasperated Voice:

So then I think: "Oh, great! Now I have an egg creature. Now this disgusting thing is out. And it's mine! What am I gonna do with it?"

(Sound of escape: sssshhhhhhh!)

Blue Flash Voice:

Sssssshhhhhhh! It bolts for the door. Ssssssssshhhhhh! Out of the shack. It doesn't have feet but it just goes "sssssssshhhhhhh" out into the night. And disappears into the Nowhere-land of Pennsylvania killing people wherever it goes. I don't know how I know it, but I just know it's out killing people. And there's nothing I can do about.

(Demonstrating Creature killing)

Creature:

Arrrrrgggggghhhhhhh! Arrrrrrrrgggggggghhhhhhhh!

Ripping Voice:

Sort of like the scene in Alien where this mouth comes out and just rrrrrrrrrrrrrrips into everybody. I know that's what my Egg Creature is doing.

Exasperated Voice:

Just my luck. Now what the hell am I gonna do about this Killer Slime?

(Pause)

Matter-of-fact Voice:

The next thing I know, it's morning and I'm in the car with my older sister Magnolia. And there's this posse or something out after the Egg Creature. And Magnolia says:

Serious Magnolia:

There's this thing out there and we gotta kill it, Theodore.

Angry Teddy:

Theodore . . . ? Theodore!? That's what she calls me when she's acting real adult with me. "We gotta kill it, Theodore." It's so phony: boy it makes me mad. But of course I stuff it and say: "Yea, right." 'Cause I know the thing is mine, and I don't want her to know that it's mine.

Serious Magnolia:

There's this thing out there and we gotta kill it, Theodore.

Angry Teddy:

(To the audience)

Yea, right.

(Pause)

Surprised Teddy:

So then I'm back in my shack. It's nighttime. And this thing comes back. My Egg Creature just appears at the door.

(Purring like the Egg Creature)

Purring Creature:

Rrrrrrrrrrrrrrrrrr

(To the Egg Creature)

Scolding Mother Voice:

Well, it's about time. You know you're causing me a lot of problems. I hope you appreciate that. Jeez. Well, I've had it with you. Get into the closet.

(Holds open the closet door)

Go on. Git! Git!!!

(Closes closet door behind the Creature)

And stay there!

(Opens the door)

And don't come out until I say so!

(Closes the door)

Good night!

(Long pause. A knock is heard. Another knock)

Who the hell . . . ?

(He goes to the door; a dorky, Pennsylvania Nowhere Man appears)

PA Nowhere Man:

E–Excuse me.

Annoyed Teddy:

What the hell do you want?!

PA Nowhere Man:

C–Can I use the phone?

Annoyed Teddy:

(To the audience)

So here's this guy, right? Some local guy, right? Making small talk.

PA Nowhere Man:

I've had a little car trouble . . .

Annoyed Teddy:

(To the audience)

And he wants to use the phone or something?

PA Nowhere Man:

I think it's my carburetor or something . . .

Annoyed Teddy:

(In disbelief)

I'm in the middle of nowhere and I'm receiving a visitor?

PA Nowhere Man:

Gee, cozy little shack you've got here . . .

Annoyed Teddy:

(To PA Man)

Excuse me, but do you mind . . .

PA Nowhere Man:

Reminds me of my old fishing shack on the Susquehanna . . .

Annoyed Teddy:

I'm sorry but I'm very busy!

PA Nowhere Man:

Do much fishing around here, do you?

Very Annoyed Teddy:

Will you get out of here, for chrissake!

(Sound of the Egg Creature)

Ripping Creature:

Arrrrrrrgggggggghhhhhhhh. Too late! The closet door flies open. And there's the thing. Arrrrrrrgggggggghhhhhhh!!!

Dumbfounded PA Man:

And the guy just looks at it with his mouth hanging open.

Matter-of-fact Teddy:

And I just turn to the guy and say:

"Do you want to be killed alive, or what?"

I say it, just like that, like it serves him right for bugging me.

"So: do you want to be killed alive, or what?"

Ripping Creature:

Boom! I mean, instantly, this guy is out of there and this thing is chasing him. Sssshhhhhooooo! Sssshhhhooooo!

PA Nowhere Man:

(Screaming)

Arrrrrrgggggggghhhhhhhh.

Laughing Sliming Teddy:

(Laughing)

And this thing gets ahold of his back and rips a good chunk of flesh off right in the middle of his back where all the flabby muscles sort of bunch up.

(Laughing)

I—I don't know why I think this is so funny . . .

(Laughing harder)

But the guy keeps running and this thing keeps running after him. And there it is again, out killing people all over Pennsylvania.

Annoyed Teddy:

So now it's pretty obvious to me that something has to be done. So we have a meeting in some attic, a brand new attic, with new paint and no furniture. It's a little vague but my sister is there, calling me Theodore, and the Sheriff is there with some indifferent deputies and they're asking me about this thing.

Proud and Unapologetic Teddy:

Finally, I hear myself saying, "Yes."

(Pause)

"It's my thing."

(Pause)

"Yes. The thing belongs to me."

(Pause)

"But what can I do about it? It may be my thing, but it's not my **fault**!"

(Pause. Then, in a tone that denies any wrongdoing)

That's how my dream ended.

Part Two

CREATING THE DREAMSCAPE

Ensemble Dream Enactment

They All Want to Play Hamlet

They all want to play Hamlet.
They have not exactly seen their fathers killed
Nor their mothers in a frame-up to kill,
Nor an Ophelia dying with dust gagging the heart . . .
Yet they all want to play Hamlet . . .

—Carl Sandburg

The idea of exploring dreams by playing all the parts was inspired by a theater production I worked on a few years after my "initiation" dream. It was called *They All Want to Play Hamlet.* In this solo-performance piece, the actor, Tim McDonough, performs a one-man version of Hamlet playing all the parts: Ophelia, Polonius, Hamlet, his father's ghost . . . everybody. He also meditates on and dramatizes his own personal responses to Hamlet and to all the characters surrounding him. In the rehearsal room, I acted as the scribe, writing down the improvisations set up by director, Vincent Murphy, to explore the various personal and theatrical themes that had led Tim to want to put himself, so to speak, inside Shakespeare's "dream" of Hamlet.

There was a strangely coincidental similarity between my rehearsals with McDonough and the dream work I was doing with Bosnak, the Jungian analyst. On stage, Tim was playing all the parts, looking at the story of Hamlet through the eyes of all the characters. In Bosnak's dream groups, I was imagining all the parts, looking at dreams through the eyes of all the characters. Examining complex emotional material from multiple viewpoints was central to both disciplines.

What's more, both experiences were deeply involved with the exploration of imagery. Like images from dreams, images from *Hamlet* were examined in rehearsal for personal associations, emotional resonance, and thematic connections. Hamlet's inky black cloak, the poison that kills Hamlet's father, the skull of Yorick—all became fuel for Tim's own exploration of his life's journey, particularly as it reflected his relationship to his own father.

During this time, Tim was developing an approach to acting he called "Acting through Imagery." To shape dramatic action he would create a series of actions, an "action score," based on the images in the text. Using body, voice, rhythm, movement, and other theatrical techniques, he would live inside the script by embodying these images.

For instance, Shakespeare's imagery in the opening soliloquy of *Hamlet* became the basis for Tim's physical approach to the text: "O that this too too solid flesh would melt,/Thaw and resolve itself into a dew . . ."

To start this speech, Tim would ask the same question we would ask of any dream image: "What's it like?" What's it like to thaw and melt into evaporating dew, and by so doing, disappear? To answer this question, Tim explored various ways to make his body, his voice, his very being, "melt" and "thaw," literally playing Hamlet sliding down a wall into a puddle of melancholy and self-loathing.

. Seeing this, I realized that this kind of embodiment of imagery provides a highly specific technique for exploring dream images. As I was working so intensively with images in the theater and in dream groups, it seemed natural to try to combine the work. Dreams are packed with emotional images, perfect for training actors.[6]

So, I began using dreams to help teach acting, dividing the actors into small groups to facilitate the work in large classes. To my surprise, the actors, who had no experience in dream groups and no particular interest in exploring dreams, began having strong emotional responses to the work. I started exploring this effect with dream groups that had little or no acting training and discovered it was just as affecting for people whose only acting experience was in a Christmas pageant, a sixth-grade play, or telling jokes at a party.

By acting things out, people were having revelations, breakdowns, flashbacks, and fantasies around the dream material. It seemed that there was something about getting up on their feet, and about putting themselves back into the dream space, that freed them up and allowed them to dive to emotional depths. The dreams, of course, brought up personal material, but beyond this

---

6.   Dream Enactment is also an effective tool in training playwrights by teaching them how to write the way people naturally speak, and in training directors by teaching them how to guide a collaborative group in the creation of an original piece.

the most moving aspect of the training seemed to come from the fact that people were playing parts in one another's dreams and physically creating the dreamscapes.

In one dream group I recall, a woman had a startling experience when she found herself face-to-face in the dream space with the actress, Mia Farrow, a character in her dream. (This was Mia Farrow after her famous breakup with Woody Allen over his affair with his adopted daughter). In the dream, Mia was simply sitting at a table in a white dress and, when the dreamer approached, looked up at her. At first, telling the dream alone, her meeting with Mia Farrow did not have much emotional impact. It was just a curious encounter. But once we sat a member of the group in a chair to play Mia Farrow, things changed. When the dreamer approached, and Mia looked up, there was an electric exchange between the two women. It was all through the eyes. In that moment of eye contact, the dreamer felt bonded to Mia Farrow, as if she understood her deeply and felt her pain. And in that moment, a flood of a childhood memories swept over the dreamer—memories of betrayal and abuse.

This then is the major focus of this next part, an approach that allows you to encounter and interact with your dream figures and your dream world. In theatrical language, you could call it ensemble dream enactment; but, in simpler terms, it could be called, like the title of this book, dreaming together.

Questioning Dreams

Getting everyone to dream your dream

By telling your dream story to your best friend in a café, you can re-experience your dream in your imagination; by acting the dream out as a storyteller, you can re-experience your dream in your body as well. By using a group of dreamers to recreate the world of your dream, there is a deeper and more startling discovery to be made: you will find yourself actually inside the dream space in the presence of the dream figures.

Dreams, after all, are three-dimensional, as we have said. They take place in a garden, a mall, an airport, a castle under the sea. With the help of other dreamers, and perhaps a doorway, a staircase, a few tables and chairs, you can give yourself a sense that you are reliving the story inside the dream space. Of course, you have to use your creativity to transform a staircase into the rapids of a river, or two straight-back chairs into the cockpit of an airplane. You also have to use your imagination to transform some woman in your group into your sixty-year-old father, or a handful of actors into a raucous crowd in Times Square on New Year's Eve. But once you make this leap of imagination, there is nowhere you cannot go. When you meet the eye of one of your fellow dreamers and find yourself face to face with the gangster who has been chasing you, or the lover who has been longing for you, the experience can be surprising and revealing. And if you choose to have some-one in the group play yourself—perhaps some particularly intense aspect of yourself—you can even discover how you appear to the other people in your dream and learn to see yourself in a different way.

Let me say again that the ensemble does not have to be made up of people who are experienced in acting. It just has to include people who are willing to take instructions from the dreamer on how to stand in for the different characters, environments, objects, and actions in the dream. Embody-ing these images, the ensemble becomes more like a chorus or a group of backup singers.

What defines the ensemble as an ensemble, and not just a group of ran-dom people, is its common purpose, which is to enter one another's dreams. Towards this common purpose each member of the ensemble has to use his or her powers of empathy to walk in the other dreamers' shoes. This isn't always easy, but is usually fun.

In any case, it takes a certain amount of time and effort. The following sections outline a method to help transform your group into an ensemble, a troupe of actors, to help you re-enact your dream. It adds ensemble images to the solo narrative that you have already created in Part One. In this process, other members of your group will play key images—taking on aspects of your dream, even aspects of yourself—to amplify the most essential moments. In this way, the dream space is recreated and dream figures can be re-encountered.

Our central objective has not changed, though. First and foremost we are trying to find a way not only to re-experience the dream for ourselves, but to communicate that experience to those who are watching our work. Again, the audience may simply be other members of your group or a few invited friends—it might even be imagined—but it is important for both the specificity of the work and its depth that you are doing it, not just for yourself, but for others. This is the deeper implication of "dreaming together."

An essential first step in getting an audience to dream your dream is to get your group to dream your dream. Unless they can imagine the physical details and the emotional impact of what you experienced, they can never recreate it for an audience.

The easiest way I have found to help your fellow dream actors step inside your shoes is to let them ask questions about your dream to fill in all the blanks. Through a question and answer session, they can get all the details and subtleties. This Q & A will resemble the kind of interchange you are likely to experience in a "talk" dream group that is trying to imagine the dream clearly. Once the ensemble has fully and precisely imagined your dreamscape, it is possible to cast them in your dream, show them how to act out the images, and incorporate them into the storytelling.

Dream Q & A

Having told the dream with body and voice, and having narrated it from the point of view of all the images, you should have gotten a good sense of the dream's emotional core. Almost everyone, though, the first time through, leaves out a lot and glosses over important information. The next step is meant to fill in the gaps and in the process convey to your fellow dreamers precisely what happened.

So, now, you will tell the dream again—this time to a small group of four to six dreamers willing to be your actors—allowing plenty of space for questions and answers. This questioning can also be done with a single partner, but there is power in having questions arise from different listeners and a power, too, in trying to convey the experience not just to one person but to a group. A group of four to six is probably best so as not to overwhelm you with a cacophony of voices. This is also a good size for an ensemble of fellow dreamers to help enact the dream.

In this round, I find it best to go back to the simplest form of storytelling: describe the dream informally as if you were telling your dream at a coffee shop or around the kitchen table. You don't have to think at all about body or voice, just about recalling the images. As you tell the dream, the group will interact with you by asking questions until they are satisfied they have a relatively accurate picture of your dreamscape.

As much as possible the group should try to keep the dreamer *inside* the dream while asking questions. Group members can help you do this by not harassing you with questions but allowing the questions to slip in during pauses. Together, you all are incubating the dream. It is okay for there to be large silences while everyone simply sits with an image. If you find it helpful, you might appoint someone in the group as the image cop whose job it is to move things along if you get stuck by saying, "And then what happened?"

It is important in this work to keep the focus on the dreamer and not on the questioner. By no means should the process bring the dreamer *out* of the dream by anyone saying things like, "Oh yes, something like that happened to me" or "That's just like a dream I had" or even "I know just how you feel." That is all about the questioner, not about the dreamer. The members of your group should just ask questions, slowly, deliberately, without jumping around too much, as if they are holding each image up to the light and looking at it from all the different angles.

It may seem odd to put the questioning of dreams ahead of a chapter on listening to dreams. Clearly, the better one is as a listener the better one will be as a questioner. Still, the fact is, it's easier to be a good questioner than a good listener. With a natural curiosity, a receptive attitude, and a measure of common sense, your fellow dreamers can ask you questions as outsiders, learn a great deal about your dream and keep you focused on the imagery. A good listener, though, has to enter into the dream, see how the images resonate with one another, and sense where they are emotionally charged. This takes a lot of practice and focus. Obviously, the two—questioning and listening—go hand in hand. But if time is limited, or the group is inexperienced, you might want to focus more on how to question dreams rather than how to listen to them.

First the facts

The first kind of questions the group should ask are the obvious ones. Like a detective on a TV crime show, interrogators should be saying, "We just want the facts, m'am, just the facts."

Is it night or day? Is it hot or cold? What are you wearing? How old is the boy? Where is the light coming from? How big is the fish? How far away is the policeman?

Often the most obvious things are *so* obvious to the dreamer that you forget to mention them, assuming that the others know not only what you were dreaming but how you felt about it.

I am back in my old neighborhood.

We need to know a lot more information before we can imagine what it was like for *you* to be back in your old neighborhood. Without this information, we will most likely imagine that we are back in *our* own neighborhood.

So we ask first for the facts. Are you in the street or in a house? Are you alone or with others? How old are you?

The search for the basic facts extends to the most ordinary things. In fact, the more ordinary the place or person or object the more likely it will be that the dreamer will neglect to give crucial information.

I am in an airport.

I see my dog.

I pick up a guitar.

Is the airport vast or claustrophobic? Do you see the planes or just the crowds? Is the pace frantic or tedious? Are planes taking off or landing?

What kind of dog is it? Is it male or female? Is it standing or sitting? Is it looking at you? What is its feeling towards you?

Is the guitar acoustic or electric? Is it old or new? Is it heavy or light? What kind of music do you imagine would come from such a guitar?

These are the kind of factual questions your group should ask.

The search for the facts might even lead to the revelation of autobiographical material. Our understanding of these dream images will change radically if there are personal connections to these images which were unreported initially.

Did you fly anywhere recently? How did you feel going there?

Have you ever known a dog like this? What were your feelings about it?

Do you actually *play* the guitar? What kind of music do you usually play, and does that music have anything to do with this dream?

Sounds, smells, temperatures, and colors

Dreams are almost invariably visual, but they often are accompanied by strong reactions from the other senses that are sometimes neglected in the first telling.

As the bells were ringing, I stepped over the manure into the water. On the other side of the pond was a girl in a yellow dress.

How did the bells sound? Like jingle bells? Like church bells? How did the manure smell? Rich and fecund? Rancid and disgusting? How did the water feel? Cold and bracing? Warm and sensuous? Of what hue was the yellow dress? Bright and delicate? Dull and stained?

Even if the dreamer is not overtly aware at first telling of these other sensual responses, he can often feel their presence in the atmosphere surrounding the dream. Questioning by the group or by a partner often brings up new memories of the dream or associations to the images, which feel true.

If the city streets are busy, the dreamer might sense traffic noise even if he did not hear it in the dream. If he is in an old summer house, he might be able to smell the old, damp wood. Asking questions about sounds, smells, temperature, and color can often evoke these qualities and enrich the memory of the dream.

However, while it's good to search for subtle qualities in dreams, don't force it. The dreamer may not remember sounds, smells, or the like and should not feel he should have to make them up. Only if the dreamer spontaneously responds with a sensual impression from *inside* the dream should questioners assume that the sounds and smells belong to the fabric of the dream and not to some artificially devised story about the dream.

The subtle flavors

With images that are commonplace, or well-known either to the dreamer or to the group, it's very easy to miss some of the nuances or even some of the central qualities of the dream.

I am standing in my garden.

My father is scowling at me.

Suddenly, I find myself in Disneyland.

These descriptions of dream moments seem pretty clear and straightforward but they aren't specific enough. The problem is: when you say "garden" or "father" or "Disneyland," each person hearing you is going to think of his own garden, or her own father, or his own trip to Disneyland. To be specific about your images, you have to give them an idea of what the words "garden," "father," and "Disneyland" mean to you. Or, as I like to put it: what "flavor" garden, father, or Disneyland?

Is the dream garden fruitful, dying, overgrown with weeds? Do you have a garden in real life? Is the dream garden like the real garden or different?

What "flavor" father are we talking about here? Is this a loving father, a strict father, an angry father? Does your father in real life disapprove of you a lot? Or is his scowling peculiar to this dream? Do you know what that look on his face means?

What is Disneyland to you? Were you ever in Disneyland? Is this dream Disneyland like the one you visited, or different? Is it a place of fun, of confusion, of commercialization? What "flavor" Disneyland are we talking about?

Getting at the feelings

Dreams evoke many feelings, and dreamers often relate the major feelings that come up in a dream. But the subtleties of some feelings can only emerge through questioning.

I see this cute boy kissing a sleazy girl and I am filled with jealousy.

The teacher says I failed the test and I am so ashamed.

As the elevator goes up and up I feel disoriented and confused.

Perhaps the first question about these emotional states should be: how do you feel these feelings in your body? Is the jealousy in your heart, or your gut? Does the shame weigh you down, or make you sick? Does the confusion make you lightheaded or shaky? If you can sense these feelings viscerally, perhaps even locate them on your torso, you may have a better handle on how to embody them with body and voice when you come to enact them.

Another good question about feelings is this: do you *know* the feeling in real life or is this feeling peculiar to this dream? Everyone has felt jealous, but the dreamer might instantly recognize that *this* jealousy over the sleazy girl is just like the jealousy she felt when her first true love left her. We might find out next that the boy in the dream resembles the first true love in some way. Or it might emerge that the sleazy girl is like a colleague at work who is always a rival for the juicy assignments.

Other responses to this question, though, are just as possible. The dreamer who failed the test might say that he never felt shame like this. He was always a good student and made a point of never coming home with a bad report card. He might recognize the shame, however, not as the shame at school but as the shame he felt as a kid when he failed miserably at baseball. Or it might turn out that the shame is peculiar to the dream and interesting precisely because it is a new and unusual kind of experience.

The point is not to interpret the dream but to get at the quality of the feeling. It is not to say, "Oh, yes, I see, you're still working out the break-up with your first love or your issues with Little League." No, it's simply to associate the dream feeling with some vivid real-life memory that can identify with precision the quality of the feelings. There *may* be a relationship between the real-life association and the feeling in the dream, but it's up to the dreamer and not the questioners to make these connections.

So: if the dreamer *does* know the feeling, she should try to identify it, associate to it, and feel it physically. If the dreamer does *not* know the feeling in real life, the questioners should ask: "What's that feeling like?"

What's it like?

Dreams are metaphorical. Their power comes often from the juxtaposition of one image with another. They constantly tease us into thinking that their images have some relationship with one another and with real life. When you ask of a dream image "What's it like?" you are really inviting the dreamer to search for analogies that can make the peculiar nature of this image particular and vivid.

I pick up a cactus with a million prickles.

The dog is barking and straining at the leash.

I am wearing a really slinky dress and a lot of garish makeup.

What's it like to be so prickly? Does it make the cactus feel invulnerable, or defensive, or well-adapted?

What's it like for the dog to feel so restrained? Does it feel the injustice of the situation? Is it enraged? Or is it searching for help?

What's it like to be so garish and slinky? Is it sexy? Shameful? A cry for attention? Or liberating, like a costume party?

Often dreamers will assume we can sense by the way they describe an image that we know already how the image feels. But that's only because they are inside the image and take its quality for granted. For the listener to understand how the image feels, a dreamer has to be more specific; and one of the best ways to be more specific is by saying what the image is like.

Sometimes, too, for the image to become clear, you have to say what the image is like from different perspectives. Take for example this image:

Across the street, cut off from me, is my wife asleep on the sidewalk. This old, crooked blind man is tap tap tapping towards her, and I know he's out to get her. (See Dennis' Blind Man Dream, p. 130.)

To the husband, the blind man seems like a predator who wants to cripple or sexually assault his wife; but from the blind man's perspective, from inside the image of the blind man, he seems more like a teacher or magician who wants to show the wife what it's like to know things without seeing them, to know things on trust.

This guy (on the dance floor) is a brawler and he's having a ball brawling. He pricks them and needles them and teases them like crazy. (See Christopher's Eight Ball Dream, p. 179.)

For the people on the dance floor, the brawler is aggressive, rude, and crude. But what's it like to be the brawler? From his perspective, he's just having fun egging people on; this is his way of getting to know everyone, his way of "dancing" with them.

It is good practice when asking "What's it like?" to listen for and encourage intuitive leaps.

I am standing with my wife outside a Gothic cathedral and I can see in one corner that the foundation stone has started to crumble.

When telling this dream, the dreamer made an intuitive leap when he heard himself say: "Gothic cathedral." It flashed into his mind that he and his wife had gotten married in a very simple New England meetinghouse and that this Gothic cathedral reflects how complex, weighty, and stony their marriage has become. The fact that the foundation was beginning to crumble reflects his fear about the foundation of their relationship.

This kind of intuitive leap should not be forced through clever intellectual mind games. It should only be trusted when the dreamer suddenly recognizes a connection and knows intuitively that the comparison between dream image and real life is personal and true.

Asking leading questions

Inevitably, when someone enacts a dream they will show by their demeanor the feeling behind an image, even if they don't say it. Reliving the image, they sense its impact so strongly that they feel no need to articulate what to them seems obvious.

The big black bull snorts and looks at me.

Inside the oyster, there is a shiny, silver pearl.

Then she smiles and kisses me, a long, long kiss.

It is natural and helpful to ask the dreamer outright how it felt, and to even try to name the feeling for them, if they don't name it themselves. You might say, that bull must be scary, that pearl must be very precious, that kiss must be delicious.

But don't ask a leading question unless you are really sure you have caught the drift, and be prepared to give up your notion if the dreamer contradicts you. After all, that bull might be wise, not scary. The pearl might be an irritant rather than a jewel, and the kiss might be overwhelming rather than delicious. There is any number of possibilities.

Still, asking leading questions is helpful because it keeps the dreamer inside the emotional atmosphere and invites her to become more exact about the quality of the feelings. It even happens at times that the very act of naming the feelings for the dreamer brings those feelings to the surface and allows a dreamer, who is otherwise blocked, to experience them.

In asking leading questions it is helpful to use the vocabulary that the dreamer offers. If a cactus is said to have a million prickles, we can ask what it's like to be so "prickly" not so "thorny." If a flash of lightning is said to "illuminate" a scene, we ask what it's like to be so "illuminated" not so "lit up." The words that dreamers use may or may not be helpful in describing the image, but by keeping with their vocabulary we avoid making unintentional interpretations. We are also inviting them to stay inside the image as they have described it until it becomes clearer what their associations are.

Savoring the nectar; salting the wound

There are special images in dreams, which seem to carry a particularly large charge with them. These are magic moments with a special aura about them, a strong magnetic or repulsive quality. They may be painful, pleasurable, shameful, or ecstatic. We can identify these moments by how fascinated the dreamer seems to be, or how much they *don't* want to talk about them. Sometimes the listener, observing how the dreamer avoids these moments by sliding over them, may become aware of how special these images are even before the dreamer realizes it.

In any case, whenever we come across these highly charged images we will probably want to hold the dreamer in them. For the pleasurable moments we might call it "savoring the nectar." This is often harder to do than it seems. In real life we are not used to, and often are not allowed to, savor the nectar. A kiss in a dream might be exquisite; but in waking life it might seem illicit or lewd or overwhelming, and there might be a lot of sexual excitement, embarrassment, or shame around it. Only by asking for details of the kiss can we keep the dreamer from popping up to waking life and commenting on the moment.

Similarly, there may be painful moments in the dream that are so painful and excruciating that the dreamer wants to flee from them. The listener might want to flee from them as well. Our job as listeners, though, is to keep the dreamer inside the dream. This requires us to put "salt on the wound" by asking for details.

I look down at my arm and see I have a wound festering with maggots.

We have to ask about the maggots. About the pus. About the pain. We have to get interested in the festering wound and not be afraid of it.

I saw my son flailing in the water gasping for breath but I couldn't save him.

We have to ask to see how the boy gasped, how he flailed, and how it felt to be helpless to save him as he went under. This may bring up strong feelings in the dreamer, maybe even tears. But as long as the dreamer can stay inside the image and answer questions about it, it is usually safe to say that this is good work, and safe work, even if painful. This is often a re-experience of the dream at the deepest level, and the most satisfying for the dreamer as long as he is prepared for the power of his own experiences.

Sometimes the dreamer will present a particularly pleasurable or painful moment in a very matter-of-fact way. And indeed it does happen that things that would be exquisite or excruciating in real life *are* matter-of-fact in dreams.

There is an orgy going on in my kitchen.

The goldfish is flopping on the living room floor.

These images might be completely natural in a dream and as empty of strong emotional content as eating breakfast in the kitchen, or seeing a goldfish swimming in a bowl. But if you, as the listener, sense intuitively that the orgy is actually incredibly sexy or that the goldfish is suffocating on the floor, you might want to call for all the details of the image to see if the dreamer has been unwittingly avoiding the powerful impact of these moments.

Savoring the nectar and salting the wound are skills that are only possible to practice if there is a good amount of trust between dreamer and questioner. It should be done delicately, using a lot of common sense about just how far to go. But it can't be repeated too often that the questioner's job is to keep the dreamer inside the dream, particularly in moments that are emotionally charged. The dreamer can always decline to answer or can request to move on, but the questioner should not be the one to shy away from these strong images. Use your questioning skills to keep the dreamer contemplating these magic moments.

However, since all of this depends on the group maintaining a great deal of trust, here are some common-sense rules that will help maintain a sense of safety.

Rule #1: The dreamer is in charge of the process at all times and can always pull out of telling a dream if he feels vulnerable or overwhelmed.

Rule #2: The dreamer can decline at any time to answer a question if it seems too personal.

Rule #3: The dreamer should try to avoid using the real names of people in the dream if members of the group know these people.

Rule #4: Everyone should agree that they will not gossip about the dream material outside the group.

Slowing it all down

In general, the role of the ensemble in this round of dream telling is to slow things down by asking questions. This accomplishes two things: on one hand, it gives everyone the opportunity to get all the details and to view the dream from many different angles; on the other, it allows the dreamer to stay inside the dream, particularly inside those moments that are mysterious or loaded with feeling.

The bull picked me up on his horns and lifted me over the fence.

"Picked me up on his horns" is too quick for such an important and complex moment. Ask about how the horns felt, the speed and power of the lift, the intention of the bull. Ask as many questions as you can think of to keep the dreamer in the moment of being lifted up by the bull.

It is not that the answers are necessarily so significant, although they might be. What is of primary importance is that the questions are framed in such a way as to keep the dreamer inside the dream.

A therapeutic dream group might take two hours for one dream. For the process of Dream Enactment, you might want to take only about a half hour per dream. This is because the process of rehearsal will bring more details to the surface. Use common sense with epics and fragments: don't search for unnecessary details in a short dream, or bog down in details when there is an enormous amount of action. Similarly, if you have a limited amount of time, or an inexperienced group, you might want to ask extensive questions only about the images that seem the most important. Whatever the level of commitment to questioning, encourage everyone to gravitate towards points in the dream that appear to have a strong emotional charge, not only for the "I" narrator but for other characters in the dream.

Listening to Dreams

The dream means what it says

The first rule of thumb in listening to dreams is to take them literally, at face value. Even if the images seem strange in waking life, or seem redolent with symbolism, accept them as facts.

I looked in the mirror and I had no face.

It is important to accept that the dreamer here is without a face in the mirror, and to find out precisely the nature of this facelessness. It may be that, as you all work on the dream, you discover that the dreamer feels anonymously "faceless" or has "lost face" or "can't face something." But at the start, don't jump to conclusions; simply find out exactly what the dreamer sees in the mirror. You might say to yourself: facelessness is happening, let's find out what kind.

There was a polar bear sitting in my bathtub.

The polar bear is a polar bear; the bathtub is a bathtub. The bear may be in the bathtub because he wants to get wet, or keep cool, or it might simply be a comfortable place for a bear to sit; but it is a particular animal in a particular place. It is not an elephant, not a mouse. It is not a kitchen, not a bedroom. You might even say to yourself: polar bear is happening, bathtub is happening, and hold the two images up to the light side by side.

Avoid generalizing, though. You may have heard about bears in myths, you may have read about bears as archetypes, you may even have your own personal associations with bears. But as a listener I like to look first at this creature primarily as a particular bear, a particular *polar* bear to be exact, and find out who he is and what he wants. The bathtub, too, is a particular bathtub. It is "my" bathtub, and you want to find out what it's like for this particular polar bear to be in "my" bathtub.[7]

By taking the dream at face value, assuming it means what it says, you will avoid getting caught in the superficial humor of dreams. Some dreams are genuinely funny. But often people will simply laugh at the strange juxtaposition of images—images that are only funny from a daylight perspective—out of a discomfort at really entering into the world of dreams. From inside the dream, it might not be funny at *all* to see yourself faceless in the mirror, or to find a bear in your bathtub.

Following both the narrative and collage

Usually we tell dreams linearly, as if they were a movie or a story. Sometimes the narratives seem to have some kind of coherence: a character development, an image that transforms, a dramatic build to an emotional climax. More frequently the dream is remembered as a collection of images, a series of scene fragments, with seemingly unrelated juxtapositions. The fragments themselves are concrete and coherent, but then the scene shifts abruptly.

It is impossible to say whether the coherence in a dream is imposed upon first waking or actually exists inside the dream, so don't even try to figure this out. Just accept the coherence (or lack of it) as part of the structure of the dream.

However, because most dreams are remembered both as a narrative and as a collage of images, they have to be listened to in both ways. Some dreams do seem to have a progression and a story line. Others are like pictures at an exhibition. Whatever form the dream takes, it is always a good idea to consider it in both ways: narrative and collage. In fact, the stronger the dream comes across as a coherent story, the more important it is to look at it as a collage,

---

7. A note on archetypes: Knowledge of myths, archetypes, and cultural symbols can be helpful in listening to dreams and understanding them in a larger context. But just as often it can be misleading. You may have read of mirrors in fairy tales or of polar bears in Inuit myths. But these may or may not be relevant to the particular mirror or bear in the dream. If a myth or symbol intuitively pops into your head, keep it in the back of your mind and see if it is relevant as you learn more about the dream; but don't offer this insight up to the dreamer. It will just take her out of the dream itself.

comparing the images. Similarly, the more it appears to be a collage, the more important it is to look for progressions, through-lines, and imagistic development, as if the dream hints at a hidden story.

For instance, in my Initiation Dream it would seem at first blush that there is a simple narrative being told:

> *I bring a precious shell up from the bottom to show my friend, a storm begins to gather and I swim for the beach, and then I am "petrified" and "illuminated" in the flash of lightning.*

This dream is more interesting, though, if the showing of the precious shell is considered simultaneous with the lightning storm rather than as a separate chapter in the story. That is, from a collage perspective, the storm is engendered by the precious shell and the precious shell is engendered by the storm. Precious things may bring up stormy feelings, and stormy feelings may bring up precious things. The two go together and belong in the same exhibition.

Listening for themes, shapes, puns

For both narrative dreams and collage dreams it is sometimes helpful to step back and ask on the most basic level what seems to be happening. Not the story line so much as the major theme or themes. Something is dying in the dream, let's say. Or something is being fixed. There is something suffocating about the dream, perhaps. Or something extremely erotic.

Even more abstractly, the geography of the dream or the environment or even the color scheme might be a significant unifying item. There may be, for instance, a movement upward in the dream with the first scene starting in a basement, the second scene climbing a mountain, the third scene in orbit on the space shuttle. In another instance, you might see that every scene has water in it: a polluted, muddy puddle, which leads to a mighty stream, which opens up to the vast ocean. In still another, the dream may alternate between very dark scenes and very bright scenes, inside and outside, whites and blacks.

It might be helpful, when such abstractions seem important, to give the dream a title, which identifies the unifying theme: "The Moving Up Dream," "The Water Dream," "The Dark and Light Dream." Such abstractions are helpful in making a road map of a dream and giving shape to the Dream Enactment.

These abstractions are not as unusual or arbitrary as you might imagine. It is in the nature of dreams to create imagistic correlatives out of psychic material. In fact, dreams are *so* literal that they sometimes make strange puns out of emotional states or social interactions.

One dreamer who feels, in real life, that everything is out of control, finds herself walking through a field of disembodied body parts. In the images of the dream pun, she is "falling apart." Another dreamer who is worried about how much pot she is smoking has a dream of getting woozy as she takes the elevator to the top floor of a skyscraper. She's getting "too high." Another dreamer, accused by a co-worker of being conceited, finds himself in a dream gnawing at the flesh of his arm, which tastes like birthday cake. In other words, he's "full of himself."

To put it another way: if there's a storm in a dream, you might wonder if things have been stormy for the dreamer lately. If there's a lot of construction going on in the dream, you might wonder if something needs fixing or mending in the dreamer's life. And if someone dies in a dream you might wonder if the dreamer has recently experienced the "death" of some wish or belief or ambition. Thinking in terms of dream "puns" helps you take the dream images metaphorically rather than literally.

Sensing the pressure

Even if the dream doesn't provide you with a theme or title or pun to help you focus on its central metaphors, by listening carefully and intuitively you may be able to feel your way to the heart of it. Dream Q&A sessions such as we have been describing are like diving expeditions. By slowing down the process with questions, and looking at the images from many different angles, the group invites the dreamer to go deeper and deeper into the dream. As he goes deeper, the dreamer will often feel a pressure building up, a psychic or emotional pressure. In fact, it often feels as if the whole group has submerged itself in the depths of the dream.

In such a state, it is sometimes possible to sense very subtle shifts of feeling and to pick up unspoken emotional nuances. By tuning in to these vibrations, you can often get an intuitive sense of what is driving the dream.

Sometimes the pressure seems greatest at obvious points in the dream— places of intense emotion or confrontation. Often though there will seem to be a lot of pressure around an image which, on the surface, has no obvious charge: a rabbit, a rusty gate, a call to come to dinner. By noticing the intensity of the pressure, and coming back to these moments in the questioning of the dream, you can often find powerful images that might have otherwise gone unnoticed.

A dramatic example of an ordinary image holding a lot of pressure is recorded in the dream play *Dreaming with an AIDS Patient* when Christopher, who is struggling with AIDS, has a fragmentary dream about eating a pomegranate. It's just a pomegranate, an ordinary pomegranate, but it chills him to the bone. On waking, he is reminded of the myth of Persephone, who was doomed to live in the Underworld because she tasted some pomegranate seeds. Christopher, facing his mortality, felt the pressure from the image of the pomegranate in his dream before his association to the image became conscious.

In all dream work you might want to start where it's easiest to enter the dream and work your way towards images that have more and more pressure. This is the process of "diving" into the depths of the dream. Becoming sensitive to the pressure in dreams, and learning how to help the dreamer dive to the greatest depths, takes practice and cannot be learned overnight. But what you *can* do from the very beginning is to slow things down sufficiently, allowing big pauses in the questioning to feel the nuances as the pressure builds up.

Questioning the dreamer and listening closely to the details of the dream prepares the whole group for Dream Enactment as an ensemble. Hopefully, by the time you have finished the Q & A session, everyone in the group will have a handle on the dream as it was experienced by the dreamer and will not be so prone to interpret it or imagine it from their own perspectives.

Taking it all personally

Perhaps the greatest gift you can give the dreamer is to listen to the dream as if it is all happening to you, as if you are not only the dreamer but all the images as well: the dreamer being chased, and the dark figure chasing; the murky pool, and the snapping turtles in the depths. Taking it personally allows you to enter into the imaginal space, feel the emotional fabric of the images, and empathize with the dreamer.

The empathy part is most important. You have to shift out of your own autobiographical reference points and enter someone else's imaginal world as if it were your own.

If you take everything personally in this way, you will be more attuned to the numinous, magical moments in dreams as well as the resistances in dreams. There will be some images that you are naturally attracted to and others that you will find repugnant and wish to avoid. Sometimes, of course, the attraction and repulsion will have more to do with your own association to the images than the dreamer's. Be prepared for this and determine, through careful questioning of the dreamer, whether you are really tuned in to the images or to your own interpretation of them. The more you can listen from an empathetic personal perspective, the more likely it will be that you can imagine what it was really like for the dreamer to be inside this dream.

In such a receptive state, you may be able at times to sense significant emotional moments that even the dreamer is unaware of. He may, for instance, mention in an off-hand, matter-of-fact manner that there is a door in his dream bedroom that isn't there in real life. You, on the other hand, will feel a great danger in opening that door. By asking questions about the door, and putting the dreamer's attention on it, you may allow him to become aware that he definitely does *not* want to open it. This may lead to a whole series of scary associations that he would not have considered if you had not felt an intuitive danger behind the door.

In order to get into this receptive state of mind, it is a good idea to take a half a minute before listening to a dream to monitor the thoughts and feelings you are having at the moment, and to clear your mind of them. Then, if these thoughts or feelings come back, you can recognize them as part of your own psychic baggage and not part of the fabric of the dream. At the same time, if you have been able to clear your mind, you may be able to get important clues to the emotional fabric of the dream by monitoring the changes in your physical and emotional state. If you get sleepy during the telling of the dream—or dizzy, or sick to your stomach, or overcome with giggles—ask yourself whether these changes have been caused by some image or action in the dream. See if you can identify precisely what images or actions first triggered these responses. Physical and emotional changes may be important intuitive hints about the nature of the images and provide good clues for the direction of your questions to the dreamer.

The opaqueness of dreams

Just about everyone who tells dreams wants to know what they mean and how they are relevant to their lives. Everyone who listens to dreams quickly learns that they are maddeningly incomprehensible and tantalizingly elusive. Islands of meaning and relevance seem to emerge at times only to be swamped by waves of incoherent details and amorphous feelings.

In listening to dreams, it is important not to be discouraged by how dense and opaque they are. That's the nature of dreams. The light of daytime consciousness is not their natural environment, and nighttime consciousness is hard to embrace. Listen to dreams as if you are a visitor to a planet that is very similar to our own but where the laws of nature and logic have been altered. Of course you won't understand everything. Don't try. Just navigate as best you can from image to image to find out what's happening there. In other words, don't ask what dreams mean but rather what they *are*.

As mentioned earlier, there are time-honored traditions in many cultures including our own that dreams are messages from the gods or from some inner voice, maybe even prophesies or visions. Contemporary dreamers also say they feel that dreams carry important life lessons: I should break up with my lover; I should change my job. While this is a common conception—I often feel this about my own dreams—it can be tricky to approach dreams as if their purpose can be known. That approach makes it too easy to slip past the images themselves in order to look for their higher purpose. Particularly with painful images, it can be an easy way to avoid feeling the feelings, comforting ourselves with the idea that ugly, sad, confusing, or humiliating images are useful for our growth or transformation.

Still, so many people feel that dreams are purposeful that we cannot ignore this impulse. You might want to treat it—the sense that the dream has a message—as an image, like the feeling of anticipation, or the feeling of dread. The feeling of purposefulness is an important quality and can be very potent. You can then ask, "What's it like to feel this dream has an important message for your life?" The quality of the urgency may then emerge.

This attitude may be important for dreamers who have frightening dreams that seem prophetic: a car crash, or a disease. If they approach this prophetic feeling as part of the image, it should be less frightening to work with because it is not taken literally but metaphorically.

In every group there's bound to be someone who says with complete candor that they had a "foreshadowing" dream that came true. We have no reason to doubt this is so. But, for the purposes of this work, I find it best to treat the prophetic nature of a dream as just another attribute of the image, leaving the larger questions of precognition to psychologists, theologians, and philosophers.

Creating an image score

During the questioning of a dreamer, it is important to have someone act as the scribe to take down all the details of the dream. It is very common for narrators to take many short cuts when acting out dreams and to ignore simple background information such as type of weather and time of day. The question and answer period will bring out these details, which are expected to be included in the narration the next time the dream is put on its feet.

For example, the dreamer might say at first that she was "flying." But on questioning it becomes clear that the flying was more like floating on her back, like the time she had floated in the Dead Sea, and that it was accomplished by simply moving her eyes up or down, left or right. These nuances—floating,

Dead Sea, eye movements—should then be incorporated into the narrative.

The scribe is not, however, trying to write out a script. Rather he or she is making a checklist of images, which the dreamer can then incorporate into a spontaneous narrative, a detailed image score. As the dream develops further with the entire ensemble participating in the enactment, this image score can grow and evolve into a complete blueprint of the narrative, an outline for performance.

Include in this detailed image score any vivid phrases that come out in the questioning, particularly ones that are idiosyncratic and peculiar to the dream teller. Ultimately, we want the voice of the narration to sound natural, as if the dreamer is simply telling us her experience. But "natural" does not come naturally to everyone. It takes a concerted effort to avoid sounding artificial or "actor-y." So if the scribe can pick up the natural phrases of the dream teller and incorporate them into an image score, that will help create a natural voice.

Here, for instance, is a possible outline of an image score for the beginning of Teddy's Egg Creature Dream (*see p. 77*) up until the moment he realizes the Egg Creature belongs to him.

Image score: Teddy's Egg Creature Dream

> *Hate Pennsylvania.*
> *Foggy, rainy, lonely.*
> *People stupid, rude.*
> *Nowhere.*
>
> *Nowhere shack.*
> *Run down. Cluttered.*
> *"Not a nice shack."*
>
> *Eggs. Not hungry.*
> *Eat? Why not?*
> *(Crack egg.)*
>
> *Blue flash.*
> *(Explosion.)*

Blinding Light.

A dome-shaped thing.
Slimy egg slime.
(Ripping. Gashing.)
"Like bloody gums."
(Arrrrrgggghhhhh sound.)

Pink beak teeth thing, slimes, chomps.
At first, frightened. Really gross.
(Watching. Waiting.)
No danger.
"It's mine."

Preparing to incorporate the ensemble

By the end of this Q & A session, the dreamer will have told the dream at least four times:

+   With sound and motion (but without words) to a partner.

+   With sound, motion, and words to a partner.

+   With sound, motion, and words to the group.

+   With words alone in a question and answer session with the group.

Once the question and answer is completed and the image score is given back to the dreamer, the dreamer is ready to begin the process of ensemble Dream Enactment by selecting a cast of players from the group. This involves choosing who will play key dream images, showing them how to play those images, and starting to rehearse with them to incorporate them into the narrative.

Before embarking on this process it might be helpful to recall the main thrust of what you are trying to do. Above all, you are trying to create a theatrical experience that will allow others to dream your dream. Everything you do should be subservient to helping others enter your dreamscape. This focus on communicating with an audience helps to ensure that you look for and devise precise and evocative stage images that illuminate the dream. It also helps to ensure that you stay alive to all the nuances of the images, and not just to the feelings that were swirling around you when you woke from the dream. In the process of shaping the dream for an audience, it is expected that you will find yourself inside the dreamscape once again, capable of re-experiencing the dream each time it is performed.

Creating a Rough Draft

Building a narrative/collage

Because dreams are remembered both as narratives and as collages, the presentation of dreams ought to show them in both lights. To do this, the dreamer plays the role of dramatic narrator, enacting the dream story in a linear fashion from beginning to end as it was remembered. As narrator, you will play all the parts, evoke all the settings, embody all the objects, perform all the actions just as you did for your partner during solo presentations, just as you have practiced up until now.

The only significant difference for you, the dreamer, will be the presence of other actors, a small ensemble, who will also embody the key images in your dream. This is the collage aspect of the dream play. It is not that they will take over these images and leave you to just play yourself in the dream. On the contrary, you still have to play all the parts so that, if for some reasons your ensemble doesn't show up on the day of performance, the audience will still receive all the dream images.

The role of the ensemble is to amplify key images, holding their essence, allowing them to resonate throughout the presentation, while you continue to tell the dream. They help create the landscape and soundscape of the dream, shape the topography of the dream space, and define the physical relationships between the images. They help compare and contrast key images. They introduce key images, perhaps before the narrator mentions them, and echo key images perhaps after the narrator has experienced them. Best of all, they allow the narrator to interact with her own dream, even her own image.

Here is a dream in strictly narrative form that would benefit from an ensemble approach to the collage of images.

Danny's Dolphin Dream

Around the time I was struggling to find a new direction for my artwork, I had a dream of a dolphin who was sick and dying. In this dream I am in a theater and the actors are getting ready to rehearse. And they are all very stuck-up and full of themselves. And on the ground in front of them is this dolphin. He is out of water and I know this is not a good thing. He is completely dry. He is drying up. And nobody seems to care.

(An excerpt—see p. 140 for the full dream.)

To perform this dream, it might be appropriate to have some of the ensemble play stuck-up actors, totally self-involved, while one actor might play the dolphin, all dried up. The narrator would still embody the image of the stuck-up actors, and the dolphin, too; but the ensemble would echo and mirror these images. Because the ensemble is mirroring these images, when the narrator plays the dolphin, the image of the stuck-up actors is still present, and when he plays a stuck-up actor the dolphin is still present.

So the first thing you have to do to provide roles for your ensemble is to decide the most potent images. Key characters will be obvious choices. Equally potent though for some dreams are the environments, the key actions, or even at times a thought, a sensation, or a geographical direction.

Take this dream:

Dennis' Blind Man Dream

And then the scene shifts and I'm in the car with my wife and . . . Whoooaaa! We are driving over a drawbridge, only . . . Ohhhhh! We're going straight up and down. Whoooaaaa! This bridge is a sheer wall! It's completely vertical and as thin as a Parliament cigarette box. Ohhhhh! We're going straight up the side. Up up up. And then . . . Whoooaaaa! Straight down again. Down down down. And I turn to my wife in amazement and say: "We've never done *this* before!"

(An excerpt—see p. 130 for the full dream.)

In this fragment, going up and down is such a striking and important part of the dream that it seems worthwhile to keep it echoing. Perhaps someone in the ensemble first lies on her back in a driving pose looking up and chanting "Up up up" and then jumps into a driving crouch looking down, chanting "Down down down." Or perhaps two actors perform these moves, alternating up and down so that always one is going up while the other is going down. If they do this over and over in a kind of a loop of sound and motion, the sense of up up up and down down down will keep echoing through the dream. This work might even be interrupted occasionally by other members of the ensemble interjecting: "We've never done *this* before!"—which could keep the audience thinking about what it's like to do something dangerous with your spouse that you've never done before.

You might notice from these examples that the role of the ensemble as an echo and a resonator is more like music in some ways than drama. Indeed, for the collage of images to surround the narrator like a chorus they have to be orchestrated.

What follows are some principles for shaping and orchestrating the ensemble images.

Casting and coaching the images

To cast people to play the images in your dream, use your intuition. Rather than choose on the basis of superficial appearances, try to find someone whose personal qualities have some affinity with the image. Women can play men, young people can play older parts, black people can play whites and vice versa, and of course anyone can play the storm or the alligator or the sound of the meat cleaver. What's important is to pick someone who can best embody the image.

In coaching the ensemble on how to act their parts, don't tell them—show them. You are the expert in your dream; you know what it was like. To tell them to get fiercer, or sexier, or sloppier only gives them a general sense of what you want, and actors need specifics. So show them how the image moves, how the image sounds, even what the image says. The actor will mirror what you do and echo what you say. In the Dolphin Dream above, you have to become the stuck-up actors, showing how they held themselves aloof, how they ignored the poor dolphin. In the Blind Man Dream, you have to become the driver going up up up and down down down so the ensemble members who are playing the parts can feel the intensity and the rhythm of the action.

If possible, assign roles; don't ask for volunteers. As the expert on your dream, you have to be guided by your vision of the dream rather than by the ensemble's preferences. It is also important to remember that, as the expert on the dream, you are the expert on how to act it out. You don't need to have experience in acting, you just need to be true to the experience of the dream. Acting will happen. And the more you trust in this, the more your fellow dreamers, whether they are trained as actors or not, will have confidence in creating images true to your dream because they will simply be trying to imitate you, reflecting your vision.

Shaping the images

The physical shape of each action performed by your ensemble should be relatively simple and repetitive, like the images explored in the warm-up circle exercises. The action could be an evocative movement (like the waving of trees) or an abstract movement (like a portrait of dread) or a literal movement (like the playing of dice). Whatever it is, it ought to loop around so that the actor can repeat the action over and over. Later, when the actor is playing the image alongside the narration, he might vary the repetitive action, letting it grow or diminish in intensity to complement the story, or even transform into variations on the theme as the dream progresses. At first, though, keep it simple so the ensemble member can get inside the rhythm, tone, and movement of the action.

In terms of sound, even if the image didn't make any noise in the dream, you probably want to give it some voice in the enactment so that it doesn't remain lifeless or static. The dolphin in the Dolphin Dream, for instance, might make a soft whimpering sound to show how dry and parched he is. The dolphin might even say (though the creature never actually spoke in the dream) "water . . . water . . ." in a pathetic, desperate voice to show its inner need.

To be specific, many images need not only sound and movement, but words as well. The stuck-up actors will remain caricatures if they have to mime being stuck-up. But given a few snooty lines they can be very animated: "Does my hair look alright?" or "This play is so superficial" or "Oh my god we're not doing the Dolphin Dream, *again!*" We should understand from the narrator that these words were not actually spoken in the dream but were the *kind* of things that were being said or thought.

Similarly, in the Blind Man Dream, the car going up up up the Parliament cigarette wall didn't *say* "up up up" but we understand that this was the sense of the movement. Otherwise we are just watching someone lying on the floor on their back making motor noises. As soon as the words are spoken we can imagine the urgency and focus of the action.

It is especially important to give words to characters or objects whose thoughts or intentions are known, even if they don't actually speak in the dream. If someone is chasing you it might be important to have them say: "I'm gonna bite you," or "I'm gonna kill you," or "I'm gonna kiss you," depending on the intention. Otherwise we may imagine a wildly inappropriate purpose to the chase. Similarly, if someone is playing the atmosphere of a pool of water it may be important to have her say, evocatively: "Warm, calm, tranquil water" or "Cold, dark, murky water," depending on the nature of the pool. Words humanize the characters and make them come alive; they also clarify the qualities of creatures and inanimate objects.

If you want to put words in the mouths of characters, creatures, or objects, make sure you give them more than one phrase; otherwise they will sound robotic. I like to give a couple of similar phrases and then allow the actor to improvise around them so they sound natural. So, for example, it will sound monotonous, artificial, perhaps even comic to repeat ad nauseum "I'm gonna get you, I'm gonna get you . . ." but it will probably sound sinister, frightening, and dramatic to say: "Gonna get you, gonna kill you, Run! Go on! Run! But you can't hide."

Stylizing the images

Every image needs to be shaped for dramatic presentation. No matter how literal or ordinary the action is, the process of finding the right sound and movement is a form of stylization. But many images, especially ones that are not on a human scale, need to be stylized much more than others to be effective. Forces of nature, creatures in the wild, inner thoughts, all beg to be boldly stylized so their full power can be appreciated. The rumbling of the volcano, the eagle's flight, the fierce desire in your lover's eye, need precise sounds and movements, perhaps even words, to evoke them.

If there is an animal in the dream, find the most important aspect of that creature and let the part stand for the whole: the playfulness of the whale's tail; the fierceness of the lioness' claws; the filthy gnawing of the rat's teeth. Even something like the dream orgy in your kitchen which, presumably, could be played out by a willing ensemble, needs to be stylized or it would just look silly and banal. If the orgy was really sexy in the dream, perhaps two actors could put body lotion on their hands and intertwine their fingers; or, perhaps, in extreme slow motion they could move towards a kiss that never actually completes itself. Because the narrator is describing in detail what *actually* happened, the ensemble members are free to stylize and interpret the action in a way that evokes the image and makes it specific and resonant.

One thing to avoid is picking superfluous images to embody. If there is golden morning light coming through a window, you don't need someone to embody the window. Use a real window in the room or just let us imagine it while you evoke the light with transcendent sounds and words that describe how rich and golden it is. Similarly, if the image is of a crowded city street but the important thing is what happens in the street—that someone picks your pocket—you don't have to use all of your players to crowd the stage. Just have one actor pick a pocket and let us imagine the crowded street through narrative description, or street sounds, or by using the audience as the crowd.

Placing the image in space

As you cast your dream, think again about where you want to place your images in space using the architecture of the room or rehearsal hall you are in. If the dream is in a wide-open space like a desert, use the center of the room; if it takes place in a claustrophobic elevator, perhaps use the frame of an open door. If you are in a secret hideout, hide behind a drape or curtain. If you are up against a towering cliff, face the back wall and look up.

If your dream consists of a single setting—a room in a great hall, say, or a clearing in a forest—this might be easy. However, if the dream is a travel dream, or a collage of different and contrasting scenes, you may have to either transform the settings or allow them to overlap like multiple exposures in photography. If the dream moves from the desert to the elevator, to the hideout, to the cliff, you can place someone in the ensemble in each of those locations; or you can have the ensemble expand, contract, move up, down, forward, and back to suggest each location. By simply locating different settings in the background, center stage, and foreground, you can give a sense of different spaces that overlap. And by transforming the physical configuration of ensemble and audience, you can suggest many varied locations.

The creation of the dream space is particularly important for the re-experiencing of your dream. If a door in your dream was on your left, place a door on your left. If you watched your lover disappear down the distant train tracks, place yourself as far as you can from the actor who plays your lost love. If you looked over a deep pool, find a rug or cloth to represent the water. And if you were trapped in a circle of savages, place the audience in a circle around you. The spatial arrangement will often trigger a visceral response to the dream, allowing you to drop into the dreamscape and discover more details as you imagine that you are really there.

Running a rough draft

Now that you have cast the dream and placed it in space, it will be helpful to rehearse a very rough version with the ensemble. It will be a mess—expect it. It won't feel like your dream—that will come later, after you rehearse it. This rough draft rehearsal, though, will give you and your ensemble a chance to try the dream on, feel it out, get a sense of the space and the relationships between the images.

The most important thing is for everyone to listen to one another, for everyone to hear the dream and sense their role in the presentation. Good acting with heartfelt emotional commitment need not happen yet. It's as if you're trying on a coat for the first time to see if it fits.

As the narrator of your dream, you'll discover that there are times you naturally want to interact with the images, and other times it seems more natural to interact only with the audience while the images appear around you. Ensemble members in turn will get a sense of when to be active players in the dream or when to be more like a back-up chorus. Inevitably, you'll find there are some moments when you should throw the focus onto the ensemble images to allow them to establish themselves. The ensemble, in turn, will discover that there are moments when they should throw the focus back to you, back to the main action of the narrative.

Aside from the obvious need to make sure the audience can hear everything, "throwing focus" is a lot like conducting music: Which "instrument" (that is, which performer) should be heard in the foreground and which in the background? When should they interact, overlap, or play off of the narrator? When should one voice leave off and another begin?

After this first run-through, you might very well want to consolidate images—getting rid of those that don't serve the dream and giving focus to those that have a strong impact. You might also be able to determine how and when an image builds and fades. And certainly the spatial relationships between the images should become much clearer through this first run-through.

Ensemble Rehearsal and Performance

MTV-style of presentation

In keeping with the notion that dreams are both stories told around the fire and pictures at an exhibition, I find it helpful to perform them in a very "presentational style." The narrator speaks out to the audience. The images speak out to the audience. Occasionally, narrator and image interact with one another; and occasionally dream scenes are played out as remembered. Most of the time, though, I like to avoid looking as if we're about to drop into a traditional drama. Most dreams won't sustain a realistic dramatic style and will just come across as phony if you script them like a play.

Of course, there are many different ways to present dreams dramatically, and you can use any theatrical style that conveys your dream experience; but to give equal weight to both the collage and narrative quality of dreams, I like to use what I call an MTV-style of presentation. On MTV, the rock videos often show the rock singer in a studio or on a stage singing the whole song. Then, interspersed with the song, they intercut different film clips that resonate with the main song—a horse galloping in a field, a girl waiting for the phone to ring, waves crashing on the beach. The main singer completes the whole song but the intercut pictures focus the eye on key images that echo the song's emotional core. Like the rock singer, the dreamer will perform the whole score, the dream narration, while the ensemble picks up on the most dramatic moments to intercut or overlay key images.

Or, to put it another way, the style of presentation is like the bank of television monitors or projection screens in a TV newsroom. The main projection screen shows the narrator telling the whole dream story, while other monitors pick up on key images—sometimes taking a wide-angle overview of dream environments, sometimes closing in on a detail of the look in a character's eye or the gun in their hand. Of course, the "monitors" or "screens" we are talking about here are the performers themselves, using body and voice to create a collage of images.

I make this analogy to emphasize how useful it can be to play the dream images directly to the audience in a presentational style. These are pictures at an exhibition, indeed. This not only simplifies the production but stays truer to the dream than would a dramatic presentation, which would pretend that dreams are causal or coherent. More importantly, playing the images directly out to the audience puts the audience in the perspective of being the viewer of these images. So, for instance, if there's a killer slowly stalking a sleeping victim, instead of having an actor stalk another actor lying on stage, you might have the killer stalk the audience, moving slowly towards them as if each member of the audience were his victim. Similarly, if there is a tender kiss, instead of having two people kissing one another on stage, you might face them both out towards the audience and have one of them show what it's like to receive the kiss and the other to show what it's like to give the kiss.

In practice, then, the dream images often echo the narrator. If the dreamer sees a dark street filled with friends who have turned into zombies, the narrator may announce this revelation to the audience: "It's the *Dawn of the Dead*." The zombies then may turn out to the audience and echo this realization in zombie voices, saying: "The Dead, the Dead, the Dawn of the Dead." Throughout the dream, the zombie army in zombie voices might also echo creepy friendly statements like "Hi, Bob, let's go bowling" or "Gee, Bob, you look like you're having a bad day." The advantage of this style is that it allows the ensemble images to continue to resonate throughout the dream. Sometimes they will be introduced before the narrator talks about them and sometimes they will continue to echo after the narrator is finished talking about them. The whole dream is in front of the audience at all times.

Of course, real dramatic moments that happen in the dream—a confrontation with your father, an unexpected reunion with your sweetheart—could be encountered as if by surprise. Again, it's like music needing orchestration: some images, like musical themes, will grab our attention while others recede into the background, until another image grabs our attention only to recede in its turn. Not every image needs to echo all the time. The art of this lies in the way you mix the narrative and collage.

Here is an example of an MTV-style presentation of a dream. In this dream script, notice that the ensemble, high up on a platform, transforms from the image of the family clinging on the cliff, to the image of the lapping waves whispering "black, white, white, black," to the image of "The Rock of Ages." Notice, too, that we hear foreshadowing of the Floating Woman before the narrator ever talks about her, and an echo of her image— "floating . . . floating"—even after the narrator has finished talking about her. This is the MTV style.

Rebecca's Cliff Dream

(*Rebecca and four members of her ensemble are standing on a tabletop in a formal pose, like a choir.*)

Ensemble Choir: (*singing*)

"Rock of Ages, cleft for me,

Let me hide myself in Thee."

(Below them, near the audience is a woman bent over with her hair hanging over her face, swaying as if floating on water.)

Echo of Floating Woman (*in a ghostly voice*):

Floating . . . Floating . . .

Rebecca (*as if clinging to a rock*): I am up on a cliff, clinging to the rock face, and my whole family is there. My mother, my father, my brother and sister.

Ensemble Family Voices (*as if slipping on the cliff*):

Mother: I'm falling . . .

Father: Hold on!

Brother: I'm losing my grip.

Sister: Cling to the rock!

Rebecca: We are really high up and I am so scared we are going to fall to our doom.

Ensemble Family Voices:

Mother: Oh, help . . .

Father: Don't let go.

Brother: I can't . . .

Sister: I'm slipping . . .

(Meanwhile, the Floating Woman continues to chant.)

Echo of Floating Woman: Floating . . . Floating . . .

(Rebecca gets down off the table as the others keep clinging to one another, slipping and crying out.)

Rebecca: Suddenly I'm down on the beach. And the sand is very white, and the water is softly lapping on the shore . . .

Ensemble Voices *(swaying, like lapping waves)*:

Black . . . white . . . white . . . black . . . white . . . white . . . black . . . etc.

Rebecca: But there are black storm clouds off on the horizon, and the contrast between the white sand and the black clouds is very intense as if they divide the world in half: black and white.

Ensemble Voices *(swaying, like lapping waves):*

Black . . . white . . . white . . . black . . . white . . . white . . . black . . .

Rebecca: I walk down the white beach, oblivious to the black clouds gathering overhead. When suddenly I see, floating in the water . . .

Floating Woman: Floating . . . Floating . . .

Rebecca: this woman rocking on the water. Listless . . . still . . .

(Rebecca floats like the Floating Woman.)

Floating Woman: Floating . . . Floating . . .

Rebecca: And something about this woman seems familiar so I wade out into the water, lift her head, and . . . (*crying out as she lifts the Floating Woman's head*) Ahhhh . . . It's me! It's my own face! Pale, white, dead.

Floating Woman: Too late. Too late.

Rebecca (*in Floating Woman's voice*): And she looks up at me with that pale white face and says: "It's too late for me."

Floating Woman: Too late. Too late.

Rebecca: "You can't save me."

Floating Woman: Don't try. Don't try.

Rebecca: "Don't try to save me."

Floating Woman (*pointing*): Them! Save *them*!

(*Rebecca looks at the ensemble up on the table, who transform back into the family, clinging to the cliff.*)

Ensemble Family Voices:

"Help. I'm slipping . . ." "I'm falling . . ." "I'm losing my grip . . ." (*etc.*)

Rebecca (*not understanding*): Save them?

Floating Woman: Save them!

Rebecca (*to the audience*): And suddenly I know exactly what she means. What the dead girl who is me means.

Floating Woman: Too late! Too late!

Rebecca: In rehearsal, it suddenly hit me. These people are all clinging to the rock.

Floating Woman: Save them! Save them!

Rebecca: And the rock is The Church. My father's Church. The Church is The Rock on which you build your faith.

Ensemble Family Voices:

"Don't let go." "Hold on! Hold on!" (*etc.*)

Floating Woman: Too late for me.

(*Putting her head back in the water*)

Floating . . . Floating . . .

Rebecca: And I have fallen so far in their eyes. I am dead to them.

Ensemble Choir (*singing*):

"Rock of Ages, cleft for me,

Let me hide myself in Thee."

Rebecca: And they are barely hanging on by their fingernails.

Ensemble Choir (*singing*):

"Nothing in my hand I bring,

Simply to Thy cross I cling."

Rebecca: And that was the end of my dream.

Interacting with images

The most significant effect of having images all around you is that, as narrator, you can enter your dream, interact with your dream, and allow your dream to surround you as you go through it, moment by moment. When Rebecca sees the floating girl she can float with her, raise her head, and, if they mirror one another, both see her and *be* her.

By creating the architecture of the dream, the narrator can actually put herself in the dream space: up on the cliff, floating on the water. Often this will result in a new perspective on the dream. In fact, it's a good idea in rehearsal for the dreamer to wander through the dream space and visit every image to see what it's like to be both part of the dream and a witness to it.

If the dream space is defined well enough, you might even be able to turn around in the rehearsal space and see what's behind and around you in the dream. In this way, you can live inside the dream space, experiencing its three-dimensional quality. While it's impossible to say whether the new details you discover are actually part of the dream or creations of your active imagination, it really doesn't matter much. Intuitively, you should be able to tell whether you are making up new information or discovering essential qualities of the dream. Don't try to fill in gaps just for the sake of seeming to know more about the dream space than you really do. But on the other hand, don't hold back new images and associations that feel important out of some notion of dream purity.

When in doubt, trust your intuition.

Echoing images

The use of echoing images deserves more attention because it is essential to the collage style of presentation. First and foremost, it allows images to appear as foreshadowing before they are introduced in the narration, and to remain after the narration has passed them by. Beyond this, echoing images can perform a number of important functions: creating dramatic tension, making connections between images, and giving a sense of resolution.

In Rebecca's Cliff Dream, the first thing we hear is a Choir singing a hymn. The first thing we see is a woman bent over, hands out in front of her, hair streaming down. We don't know why we're hearing "Rock of Ages" or why the woman is "floating . . . floating . . ." but we can feel the tension between these two opposing images and sense that the dream will dramatically reveal and resolve the connection between them.

An even more subtle use of the echo occurs with the simple repetition of "white" and "black." When Rebecca comes down to the beach, the sand is white and the storm clouds are black. Working on the dream, she realized that seeing everything in white and black was something she associated deeply and painfully with rigid Church doctrine. So, by having the people clinging to the cliff transform into swishing waves, which echo the theme "black, white, white, black," she keeps the black and white imagery in the forefront of the dream.

Dennis' Blind Man Dream is another example of a dream with echoing imagery. It has three distinct parts. The echoes tend to keep each of the parts alive while the others play out. In this way, we are reminded that the dream is really more like a triptych (a painting in three panels) than a coherent narrative. Imagine, as you read it below, that you are seeing three dreamscapes simultaneously: The Street, The Bridge, The Concert Hall.

In the middle scene, we hear of the strange car ride over the bridge that goes up up up and down down down. As discussed earlier, what seems important are the vertical directions, going up on a steep incline and then down in a precipitous fall. By having someone in the ensemble echo these directions by calling "up up up!" and "down down down!" the entire dream is informed by highs and lows. The rises and falls resonate with rises and falls of the singer's voice in the third scene of the dream, and her successes and failures at hitting her notes. The furious rushing quality of the car ride also resonates with the horizontal busy-ness of the city street in the first scene, with all the people rushing to and fro across a busy corner. I'm not sure what these directions mean, and neither is Dennis; but the up and down, high and low, to and fro quality seems important and suggests a kind of frenetic aesthetic coherence to the architecture of the dream.

Dennis' Blind Man Dream

Dream Scene 1: The Street

(The Sleeping Wife lies on her side in the street. Ignoring her, two ensemble members rush back and forth in vertical and horizontal lines, creating the sense of a busy street corner.)

Rushing Workers: It's so late. Out of my way. Hurry. Hurry. *(etc.)*

(Meanwhile, two Drivers from the second scene, The Bridge, drive at a furious pace, one on his back facing up, the other bent over facing down.)

Echo of First Driver: Up . . . Up . . . Up . . .

Echo of Second Driver: Down . . . Down . . . Down . . .

(Meanwhile, from the third scene, The Concert Hall, an Opera Singer is singing scales, preparing to perform an aria from Carmen.)

Echo of Opera Singer: Do Re Mi Fa So La Ti Do

(Back in the first scene, The Street, the only one moving slowly is a Blind Man who seems to be searching for something, tapping with his cane.)

Blind Man: Where? Where are you?

Dennis *(narrating in a rushing voice)*: I had a dream and in this dream, I'm on a busy corner. Everyone's hurrying. Traffic is streaming. People, cars, rush back and forth, back and forth.

Rushing Workers: It's so late. Out of my way. Hurry. Hurry. *(etc.)*

Dennis: Across the street, cut off from me, is my wife asleep on the sidewalk. This old, crooked blind man is tap tap tapping towards her, and I know he's out to get her.

Blind Man: I know you're out there. You can't fool me.

Dennis *(to his wife)*: Get up! Get up!
(To the audience): But she won't get up. She just lies there. Like a lump.

Echo of First Driver: Up up up.

Echo of Second Driver: Down down down.

Dennis: Oh my god, he's gonna kill her.

Blind Man: I'm no fool. I know where you are.

Dennis: Or maybe . . . *(closing his eyes like a Blind Man)* Maybe he just wants to show her something.

Blind Man: Oh, yeah, I'll show you something. There! I see you!

Dennis *(still like the Blind Man)*: He's getting closer and closer.

Blind Man: Yes! I know you're there. I know things without looking.

Dennis (*as himself*): I'm so scared for her. Oh, please, wake up!

Blind Man: Ha! Gotcha!

(He taps the Sleeping Wife with his cane.)

    Echo of Rushing Workers: Take a left, a right. Right, left . . . Hurry. Hurry . . . etc.

    Echo of Opera Singer (*a crescendo*): Do Re Mi Fa So La Ti Do.

    Echo of First & Second Drivers (*to one another*): We've never done *this* before!

Dream Scene 2: The Bridge

Dennis: And then the dream shifts and I am in the car with my wife and . . .

(Out of control)

Whooooaaa! We are driving over a drawbridge, only . . . Ohhhhh! We're going straight up and down.

First Driver: Down down down.

Second Driver: Up up up.

    Echo of Rushing Workers: Hurry, hurry.

    Echo of Blind Man (*tapping towards the audience*): I know where you are. I know you're there.

Dennis: Whoooaaaa! This bridge is a sheer wall! It's completely vertical and as thin as a Parliament cigarette box. Ohhhhh! We're going straight up the side. Up up up. And then . . . Whoooaaaa! Straight down again. Down down down.

First Driver: Up up up.

Second Driver: Down down down.

    Echo of Rushing Workers: Hurry, hurry.

Dennis: I turn to my wife in amazement and say: "We've never done *this* before!"

Everybody (*to the audience*): We've never done *this* before!

Dream Scene 3: The Concert Hall

Opera Singer (*singing* Carmen): Do Re Mi Fa So La Ti Do (*etc.*)

Dennis: And then the dream shifts again and I am in a concert hall with one of my favorite students and she is singing an aria from some intricate opera: Carmen or Rigoletto. And her notes are soaring up up up and coming down down down in a great crescendo. And I'm giving her a look of great encouragement.

Echo of First Driver: Down down down.

Echo of Second Driver: Up up up.

Echo of Rushing Workers: Take a left. Take a right. (*etc.*)

Echo of Blind Man (*stalking the audience*): I know you're there! I can feel you out there!

Dennis: But . . . Oooooo . . . She keeps hitting these sour notes. And I think, oh my god, she's failing. This is awful.

Opera Singer (*singing flat notes*): Do Re Mi Fa So La Ti Do (*etc.*)

Dennis: But then comes the climax of the aria and her voice soars up up up . . .

Echo of First & Second Drivers: Up up up and up and up . . .

Dennis: And just as it reaches its peak, she hits the most beautiful pure note.

First & Second Drivers: We've never done *this* before!

Rushing Workers: Hurry . . . Hurry . . .

Blind Man: I know you're out there! I know it!

Dennis: And I'm filled with such pride. She's done it. She's a master singer now.

Opera Singer (*singing beautifully*): Do Re Mi Fa So La Ti Do (*etc.*)

Echo of Blind Man (pointing his cane to the audience): See! This is how you know things without looking.

Dream Scene 1: The Street (Revisited)

(The Sleeping Wife suddenly wakes up.)

Sleeping Wife: Ahhh! Was I asleep?

(Everyone in the ensemble looks at her, and shouts.)

Everyone: Wake up!

(Pause)

Dennis: And that was the end of my dream.[8]

This script gives only a blueprint for how the dream might be presented with echoing images. In practice, the echoes would have more variations and would often slip under the narrative as background music. The narrator would alternate more often between playing himself (i.e., Dennis), and playing The Blind Man, The Rushing Workers, The Drivers, The Sleeping Wife, and The Opera Singer. There might even be an extended aside to the audience, when Dennis first transforms into the Blind Man, to explain how he discovered in rehearsal that the Blind Man was not necessarily trying to kill his wife, but might have been trying only to provoke her, to wake her up and make her realize that there was another way of seeing. The main point of this example of ensemble enactment is to show how, in a dream with disjointed scenes or settings, you can keep all the important images alive to form a dream collage.

Keeping the images alive

If images are going to be echoed, it's important that they not sound robotic. Especially when words are used to show the inner life of an image, they should not be repeated in a monotonous manner, but as variations on a theme. In other words, they should have a living quality. In Dennis' Blind Man Dream, the Blind Man never actually said anything; his words in performance are

---

8. In the actual dream, the Sleeping Wife did not wake up. But in working on the dream, Dennis felt intuitively that so much of it was about his desire to wake his wife up and to have her sense a new way of knowing things, that he decided to create a final image that embodied this unfulfilled longing.

understood to show his inner intention. But if he were simply to say over and over again "I'm going to get you, I'm going to get you" or "I see you, I see you" he would seem crazy rather than purposeful. And, since his intention from Dennis' point of view—that he wants to kill his wife—is different from his own—that he wants to provoke her—his language has to reflect the nuances in the dream. Conversely, for dramatic purposes some phrases can be used repetitiously—like "We've never done *this* before!"—if the phrase resonates and gains increased significance by being repeated in various contexts.

To use the earlier example of Rebecca's Cliff Dream: if the people on the cliff are slipping and afraid they're going to die, they shouldn't keep repeating like robots "We're gonna die, we're gonna die." Rather, to give them the breath of life have them repeat variations on the theme "Oh my god. I'm slipping. Hold on. I don't wanna die."

Even sentences from the dream that are clear and varied if repeated verbatim over and over will sound unnatural. So if the floating girl says "Don't save me. I'm already dead. Save the others," simply picking out phrases and varying the order will keep the image alive. "I'm already dead. Already dead. Save the others. Don't save me."

Sound and other special effects

To create the environment of your dreams, it's sometimes very effective to use sound instead of space to evoke a sense of place. Your favorite hard rock song can create a party; the whistle of wind can evoke a desolate prairie; church bells can sanctify a room; hissing sounds can create a basement filled with venomous snakes.

This is really a process of allowing a part (in this case the sound) to represent the whole. The same principle can apply to any of the senses. The smell of incense, the bubbling of running water, a mysterious red light can all be used to evoke a dream environment. Not that you should overproduce these dreams, making them some kind of theatrical extravaganza. But the judicious use of special effects can call up the right kind of atmosphere and allow for a sensuous experience of the dreamscape.

In fact, feel free to do anything and everything that can make the dream come alive. If you are enacting a dream that takes place in the Arctic, you could pass ice cubes through the audience to let them feel the cold. If some crazed psycho is chopping up body parts, bring in a steak and whack it on a chopping board with a meat cleaver. If your dream takes place in a bakery, turn on a couple of toasters and let the smell of muffins fill the room. All these special effects enhance the experience of the dream, as long as the audience knows that they are meant as associations or evocations of some image and are not the image itself.

Recurring sounds, props, costume pieces can even be used to give coherence and integrity to a dream if they are woven through the fabric of the presentation. In the dream below, a beautiful white cloth is used as a wedding gown. It transforms into the aisle of the church, the blowing white snow, and the front seat of a white limousine. It even is used as the flash of a wedding photographer's camera. Through the use of the white cloth, this dream, then, becomes The White Bride Dream, the dream of the pure white bride.

Sigvor's White Bride Dream

Sigvor, the Bride, stands beside her Groom.

Sigvor: It is my wedding day, I'm getting married.

(*She puts the **white cloth** over her as a wedding gown.*)

But I am not sure if I should do it. This man, in real life, has been married four times. And I would be his fifth wife. But he has gotten me this beautiful wedding dress. And he is very rich. I realize in the dream that, if I marry him, I could do my art without worrying about making money.

(*She pauses, considering what to do.*)

I'll take the risk.

(*She places the **white cloth** on the ground as the aisle of the church.*)

We go to the church. The priest is there. There are photographers everywhere. And they want to take our picture.

(Three members of the ensemble act as photographers. Two slap the white cloth in the air making a snap like the click of a camera, while the other takes the picture. The bride and groom freeze at each snap. She is beaming. He looks distracted.)

He looks uncomfortable and won't even look me in the eye.

(She grabs him.)

I grab him by the collar and yell: "If you don't do this properly I'm leaving."

Photographers: If you don't do this properly, she's leaving!

Sigvor: He straightens up and looks me in the eye.

*(The groom puts the **white cloth** over her head as a wedding veil.)*

Groom: I promise to love, cherish, honor, and protect you for better or worse for richer or poorer in sickness and in health 'til death do us part.

Sigvor *(simultaneously, to the audience)*: He says his vows. I say my vows. Then we walk out of the church. There is snow on the ground and it's blowing all around.

*(The ensemble runs with the **white cloth** as if it is blowing snow and places it over two chairs. The **white cloth** becomes the front seat of a white limousine.)*

Sigvor: He leads me to a white limousine. I am not sure which side to get on. He doesn't hold the door so I get in the driver's seat. He gets in the seat next to me. I have the steering wheel but he has the key and the gas and the brakes on his side. So he starts it up. And I am driving. It is very slippery and very curvy.

Photographers *(to the groom)*: If you don't do this properly, she's leaving!

*(They stand. The photographers place the **white cloth** over both their heads creating a white canopy.)*

Sigvor: But then he stops the car. He looks at me and for the first time kisses me. It is not a sexy kiss but a warm kiss, a deep kiss, and I feel very safe.

*(The photographers lower the **white cloth** in front of their faces. A bright light shines from behind, silhouetting them in a long kiss.)*

Note that in this dream, Sigvor chose not to animate the groom by giving him words to indicate his inner intention other than his vows. It seemed to her that her lack of understanding of his intentions was an important part of the dream. Instead, by emphasizing the white cloth, she chose to focus on the magic of the wedding day—its purity, elegance, and hope.[9]

Ensemble moments

Some images are so resonant they overwhelm the dream with their emotional quality: the stab of a needle in your palm; the flash of a bare leg on the dance floor. When these powerful images occur the other images in the dream seem to disappear or fade into the background. There is nothing but the stabbing pain, nothing but the voluptuous flash of ankle and thigh. Even less dramatic images can sometimes color the entire dream with their affect: a pool of water that seems so inviting; the sickening smell in the bathroom.

To highlight these moments or feelings, you can sometimes use the entire ensemble to create a collective image. Suddenly, everything else in the dream stops and everyone transforms into some aspect of that single powerful moment. Everyone is being stabbed or is driving the needle home; everyone is dirty dancing or watching the sexy moves.

If the key image is the pool of water, perhaps everyone runs water over their bare arms and says to the audience, enticingly, seductively: "Take a swim. You know you want to. Go on. Dive in." Or, at the moment the narrator goes into the stinking bathroom stall, perhaps everyone starts making retching noises. That is, the whole dream suddenly stinks.

As you will see in the Dolphin Dream that ends the next section (*see p. 140*), there is a group moment when everyone in the ensemble encourages the audience to sing "Dolphin drink water." The sound of children's voices fills the space. Perhaps the audience will actually sing along.

Using the audience

In creating the landscape of a dream, you can use the audience to help define

---

9.   Some time after this dream, Sigvor really did get married, and considers this dream in some way anticipatory of that event.

your space. If, in your dream, you pass through long corridors or winding forest paths, you can ask your audience to form a corridor or a winding path in which you perform among them. If you are surrounded by wolves, the audience can circle around you to give the impression that there are eyes everywhere watching you. If there is a war between two characters fighting over a prize, you might put some images behind the audience and some in front of them to place them in the middle of the fray.

Whatever configuration you use, it helps to move the audience around at times to change their physical orientation. This has the effect of wiping the slate clean in preparation for entering an entirely new dreamscape. If you have a lot of dreams, you may not want to do this with every dream or the audience will simply be annoyed. But for a dramatic change of theme, tone, or image, it is very effective to change the audience's physical perspective.

Another effective way to engage the audience is to have an actor walk among them whispering in their ears evocative phrases from the dream to give them an intimate, personal sense that they are actually in the dream. Take this dream moment for instance:

This hot gangster guy pulls up in his mob mobile and I know by the look in his eye that he wants me to get in his car.

To give a sense of the seductiveness of this image, you might have a member of your ensemble approach individual women in the audience, whispering sleazily in their ears: "Get in the car. C'mon, baby, get in. You know you want to. Lemme take you for a ride."

In special cases you can even involve the audience in the dream by asking them to participate. You can offer them cookies similar to the ones you baked in a dream, or ask them to stand up for the National Anthem at the start of your baseball dream: "Play ball!"

Involving the audience requires caution and common sense. The audience will be taken out of the dream if they worry that they will suddenly have to become performers. To avoid this, let them know the limits of their participation and when it will be over.

To give a better sense of how you can use the audience and incorporate ensemble moments in an ensemble dream, here is Danny's Dolphin Dream fully scripted. Note the group moment at the end when the whole ensemble amplifies the Dolphin's experience of slaking its awful thirst by drinking the refreshing water: "Ahhhhhh!" Note, too, the childlike feel to the dream. If, in the end, it's reminiscent of the moment in *Peter Pan* when the audience is asked to clap to save Tinkerbelle, that's no accident. Danny experienced the dream as if it were a child's fable so the form reflects this childlike perspective.

Danny's Dolphin Dream

One actor in gray T shirt and sweat pants lies on the floor, arms out past his head in the shape of the nose of a dolphin. Three Bored Actors are lounging about: one looks at a script, one combs her hair, one does an actor's voice warm-up, all in a very stuck-up and dismissive manner, ignoring the dolphin. The first thing we hear is the whimpering of the dolphin.

Dolphin (*whimpering*): Mmmm . . . mmmmm . . . mmmm . . .

Danny: Around the time I was struggling to find a new direction for my art work, I had a dream of a dolphin, who was sick and dying.

Dolphin: Help me . . . Help me . . .

Danny: In this dream I am in a theater and the actors are getting ready to rehearse. And they are all very stuck-up and full of themselves.

First Actor: This dream work is so boring.

Danny: And on the ground in front of them is this dolphin. He is out of water and I know this is not a good thing. He is completely dry. He is drying up. And nobody seems to care.

Dolphin: Water . . . Water . . .

Second Actor: Oh my god we're not doing the Dolphin Dream, *again*?

Danny: I don't know what to do. I bring water over to the dolphin but he is too weak and too dry to drink. I go to the actors and say: "Do something!" but they just ignore me, too involved with their own preparations.

Third Actor: Where's my hairbrush. Has anyone seen my hairbrush?

Dolphin: Help me . . . Someone, please . . .

Danny: Then I see some children—three little children, one girl and two boys—and I go to them to get their help.

(The three Bored Actors now transform into three Dancing Children and start humming the tune to the song they will sing.)

For some reason, now, the dolphin is facing in the other direction.

(Danny lies down opposite the Dolphin and takes his mirror image, arms outstretched, touching noses.)

Danny (*in the Dolphin voice*): . . . And I know it is not long for this world.

Dolphin (*in a whimpering voice*): Water . . . Water . . .

Danny: So thirsty . . . So dry . . .

Dolphin: Water . . . Water . . .

Dancing Children: Dolphin drink water! Dolphin drink water!

Danny (still lying on the ground): We make a ring around the dolphin and the children begin to dance and sing—"Dolphin drink water! Dolphin drink water!"

(The Dancing Children dance around the double image of the dolphin.)

Children: Dolphin drink water! Dolphin drink water!

(Danny sits up and strokes the Dolphin and implores the audience.)

Danny: C'mon sing it with us. We have to save this dolphin.

(They all prompt the audience to sing the song: "Dolphin drink water! Dolphin drink water!")

And the dolphin reaches out his nose to the bowl of water, and his nose becomes like an elephant's trunk and he sucks the water up, and . . .

(Danny reaches his "elephant trunk" out to the Dolphin and the Dolphin does the same.)

Ahhhh—he drinks. He drinks his fill.

(Danny makes a drinking sound. Dolphin makes a drinking sound. The Dancing Children also transform into images of the Dolphin—they make drinking noises too.)

Danny: Ahhh . . .

Dolphin: Ahhhh . . .

Ensemble Dolphins: Ahhhh . . .

Danny: And that was the end of my dream.

All: Ahhhhhhhh . . .

Part Three

MAKING DREAM THEATER

Dramatic Dream Enactment

Dreaming with an AIDS Patient

In this dream, I'm standing on the corner. It's just some corner. And I look across the street. And all I know is . . . My only thought is . . . I have to cross to the other side.

"Christopher's Initiation Dream," his first dream in analysis, from
Dreaming with an AIDS Patient

In the late 80s, my fascination with dreams and theater came together in the creation of a dream play called *Dreaming with an AIDS Patient*. Robert Bosnak was working on a book by that title about the psychoanalytic work he had done with a man named Christopher, who, in the course of his therapy, died of AIDS. He told me about his experiences with Christopher and showed me the series of dreams that Christopher had left behind in his dream notebook.

This was no ordinary dream series. And the book was not an academic exercise. The dreams had themes and images that developed and transformed through Christopher's intense struggle with AIDS. Furthermore, Bosnak was not an aloof therapeutic witness; he became deeply, emotionally involved in Christopher's journey and the book was a labor of love. Here was the stuff of drama—a complex, intimate relationship and a spiritual awakening under the shadow of death.

This work brought into stark relief an aspect of dreams that I had not fully appreciated before: that dream images often repeat themselves and transform over time. Some people return again and again to a particular landscape or a particular activity. Christopher, for instance, dreamt of beautiful queens and polluted waters and landscapes that were black and white. His initial dream in therapy, that he had to "cross to the other side," was the first in a series of dreams about "crossing over"—crossing over sexually, crossing over mortally, bearing his cross. These recurring images often transformed and morphed according to how he was feeling emotionally or spiritually in relation to events in his real life and his struggle for survival.

This seemed to me, then and now, fascinating as a theatrical experience. It is extremely evocative to see dream images come to life and real life presented in terms of stage images. The idea of following dreams that return again and again to certain themes and images opened my eyes to new possibilities in theater. This led me to introduce informal Dream Enactment shows as a regular part of the performance curriculum at Boston University, where I teach, and to culminate my Dream Enactment training workshops with dream presentations.

What I discovered was that everybody I worked with—students in an acting class, women in a women's group, therapists at a dream conference, and museum workers in Australia—had dramatic stories to tell through their dreams. This is where I realized we all have "our own Shakespearean stage" inside of us.

A few years after writing *Dreaming with an AIDS Patient,* I developed another full-length play, *The Wild Place,* based on a dream series of Susan Thompson, who gave birth to her second child while still nursing the first. Her dreams were not only moving and haunting; at times they were hilarious: dreams of squirrels eating at her house, dreams of a ravenous alligator sleeping in her kitchen. On a more profound scale, her dreams, like Christopher's, reveal something universal about human experience. You don't have to be pregnant, or even female, to appreciate the primordial, almost bestial, feelings that come up when your body is responding to its most basic instincts. In this way, we connect to a common vocabulary and grammar that bind us together through the language of dreams.

Other dream shows have followed: a collection of dreams which seems to chart a soul's journey from birth to death, for instance, or a dream series that chronicles one woman's illicit and exciting love affair. Sometimes the dream presentations are informal and varied like a cabaret, and simply provide a window into the imagination of the dreamers; sometimes the presentations are more formal and coherent, suggesting more overarching, universal themes that bind the dreams together. Whatever the form of presentation, I find Dream Theater to be, often, the best show in town.

I want to make it clear that these dream plays are in no way "dreamy" or surreal. Like real dreams, they are concrete and specific in their details. But taken as a series of images, they play, in many ways, more like music than like drama. The images tease us with meaning and evoke moods and feelings that are suggestive and provocative. Dream images and real life resonate with one another and in the end we are left with a vivid portrait of the dreamers, their inner lives and their daily lives.

The following sections, then, are a guide to the creation of your own Dream Theater—either an informal presentation to your friends and colleagues, or, if you are ambitious and theatrically inclined, the creation of a "Dream Café," a performance space, sort of like a jazz club, where you might come to hear a hot set of dreams every night.

Shaping the Dream Show

Informal ensemble presentations

The simplest form of Dream Theater is just a presentation of the dreams that your ensemble has collected at random and worked on as a group. It's sort of like a dream "show & tell." Everyone gets to present his or her favorite dream. You'll be surprised, though, to discover that these "pictures at an exhibition" brought in by different dreamers will often resonate with one another, contrast with one another, and take your audience on an emotional roller coaster ride.

Since most dreams do not have a full dramatic arc, and since most loose collections of dreams do not have a coherent dramatic shape, I like to keep this kind of dream show informal, unpretentious, and minimally produced. The audience should feel that they've come to hear storytellers talk about personal experiences rather than thespians declaiming melodramas. These are just dreamscapes revisited. By keeping the audience's dramatic expectations low, it's easier to surprise, even amaze them, at how moving and theatrical dreams can be.

In choosing the running order of the dreams, look for affinities and dissimilarities. Structure the performance like music, clustering and varying the dreams by mood and energy. We'll talk later about creating more formal and coherent dream shows; but for now, with a random assortment of ensemble dreams, consider the presentation like a vaudeville or music hall show. That is, instead of the dog act, the chorus line, the standup comic, your variety show intersperses funny dreams, scary dreams, sexy dreams, and the like.

To further outline the structure of the presentation, you might want to give a title to each dream. While dreams are generally more ambiguous than a title suggests, labeling them creates a roadmap for the audience and helps underline affinities and differences.

You might even want to make a program listing the dreams and the dreamers, like programs you see in theatrical playbills. The purpose of this is not to undercut the informality of the presentation but simply to remind the audience that they are going to see a show, not a didactic demonstration. It draws the audience's attention away from the therapeutic, analytic, neurotic, and obsessive connotations of dreams, and focuses more on a theatrical mindset that is playful, imaginative, and evocative. It reminds everyone that these are the performers' own dreams, not unlike their own, and suggests that maybe they would want to share their own dreams with one another when the show is over.

In this spirit, at the end of the show have the dream ensemble take a bow and invite some well-deserved applause. This theater ritual helps bind together the common experience of actors and audience.

The dream as life story

Since we all recognize that dreams are personal and connect in some way to our waking life, audiences will project onto the narrator stories and associations that they imagine might have generated the dream images. Sometimes these imagined stories are obvious and true, sometimes fanciful and inaccurate. But the projection is inevitable.

For this reason, if you want the audience to experience your dream, and not simply speculate about it, you have to provide them with enough information about the life story behind the dream to point them in the right direction. This is not meant as an analysis of the dream but rather as a window into its real life foundations, which may be emotionally loaded. Of course, maintain whatever amount of privacy you think is appropriate. But even the briefest glimpse into the story behind the dream will help focus the audience on your experience of it rather than on their fantasy of it.

Often this can be done with the simplest observations:

I had this dream just after I broke up with my boyfriend.

I had this dream a couple of weeks ago when I was under a lot of pressure at my job.

Such remarks might act as a preface or conclusion to the dream. It is often more evocative, though, to include real-life associations in the body of the dream.

This crazy bartender reminds me of the rock singer I saw the night before.

The barking dog looks a lot like my dog, Laddie, who died last year.

You might even choose to relate these associations as if they are occurring to you at the moment in performance, especially if such associations or insights occurred spontaneously in rehearsal.

For instance, in rehearsing The Cliff Dream (*see p. 125*), Rebecca really did spontaneously associate the rock of the cliff with the Rock of the Church. It struck her suddenly with a deep grief how her family was still clinging to the Rock of their faith while she had left it far behind. In performance, then, it was dramatic and true to the dream to present this information as a discovery.

The effort to suggest real-life content and associations is part of the rediscovery of the dream, and lends immediacy, depth, sometimes even humor to the performance. It is often the most moving part of the dream presentation. It is also one of the most delicate aspects of the presentation, since it requires self-revelation without self-indulgence. How much to divulge and with how much feeling is, perhaps, the most important aesthetic choice you have to make.

Here are a few guidelines to follow when making real-life associations:

+ Stick close to the image of the dream.

+ Don't spin off into elaborate autobiographical stories.

+ Use the vocabulary of the dream to talk about the real life events.

If the rock of the cliff reminds you of the rigidity of the Church, sing Rock of Ages to evoke that association but don't go into rambling reminiscences of growing up in the strict rules of the faith.

Present the association as its own image. In other words, don't drop out of the dream to speak of your pet dog, or your neighborhood bartender, or your family's Church as if you were a news reporter; instead, use the body language and the feeling tone you would reserve for your dog, your bartender, or your Church to incorporate them into your narrative. Give these real-life associations a body and voice which coincide with, or contrast with, the images of the dream.

Stylize the image to allow the audience to feel what you feel about the real-life associations. If the associations bring you to tears or make you laugh uproariously, find a way to show the image in a tender light, or a zany one, in order to evoke these feelings in the audience.

As most professional actors know, the easiest way to make an audience laugh or cry is often by holding back these impulses on stage and implying the feelings rather than indulging in them. Sometimes, the audience's catharsis can't happen unless you hold back your own.

Affinities and differences

In any group of dreams you will find affinities and differences. Some dreams are funny, some horrible; some are fantastical, some mundane; some are sexy, some sad. The order you put them in will determine, in large measure, the emotional journey of the audience. You might start with dreams of love and end with dreams of death. You might start with dreams of family life and end with dreams of imaginary creatures. You might cluster dreams in categories: flying dreams, childhood nightmares, dreams of sisters and brothers.

However, dreams resist categorization and manipulation. They have no obligation to be dramatic, thematic, revelatory, or cathartic. They are messy and unruly, just like life. Sometimes they give hints of meaning, purpose, structure, or character development; but just as often they tease you with elusive connections, or worse, they come across as nothing more than a series of seemingly random events.

The artist's job is to give shape to this lump of clay. If we work with dreams long enough, and watch how they illuminate the experiences of waking life, shape does start to emerge. By putting dreams in a certain order, or juxtaposing one dream with another, we can create a kind of imagistic tapestry that may have some coherence.

All the full-length dream shows I've worked on weave together reoccurring imagistic themes and create a resonance between dreaming and waking life. Being made of intimate material, they are played with a passion and immediacy that stimulates the audience's most personal reminiscences. As they contain universal, archetypal material, they explore the boundaries of our common humanity. And of course the strange juxtaposition of images opens up many possibilities for fantasy and comedy.

The shape of a dream show should not be imposed but should come out of the content of the dreams. If you assume that there is a shape to be discovered, it will probably be revealed.

Here are some shapes a dream show might take:

A period of time. One shape is temporal with all the dreams related to a contained period of time: a set of dreams harvested in the weeks after 9/11; a set of dreams of pregnant mothers about to give birth; a set of dreams of high school students on a month-long Outward Bound adventure.

A common experience. Another shape for a dream show might be experiential with all the dreams related to a common life-experience: the dreams of Olympic athletes; the dreams of heart transplant patients; the dreams of Palestinians and Israelis at the height of the Intifada.

A common theme. Still another shape is thematic, with dreams chosen for their common images or narratives: dreams of the end of the world, dreams of fantastical creatures, dreams of being a superhero. Similarly, sister dreams, sexual dreams, flying dreams could hold the show together with their common threads.

A sequence of dreams. Of all the shapes, though, the one that I find most compelling is the dream series—a sequence of dreams of a single individual in which certain images and themes transform and evolve over time. Often this transformation will accompany changes that are going on simultaneously in the dreamer's waking life. The congruence of real-life changes and dream-life transformations creates a kind of character revelation that is often dramatic and deeply moving.

The dream series

Dream images are not static, singular events; they have a life of their own and evolve over time. If you write down your dreams frequently enough you can see the same images appear and reappear, often in different guises. Sometimes it's clear that the images are transforming in response to things that are happening in real life. Sometimes these transformations have no apparent relationship with the outside world but to some internal evolution. Looking back you can sometimes see that the dream transformations actually prefigure some movement in your life, as if your interior image-maker is more aware of your life-changes than you are.

My wife, for instance, in her single days, often had sailing dreams. But shortly after our children were born she had a dream in which the Captain said: "The ship must sink." A week later, in real life, we were on a friend's sailboat, coming into port, when a freak storm knocked us down and our boat actually *did* sink. The sailing images dried up after that; but some time later, when the kids were no longer infants and were beginning to be a bit easier to handle, she dreamt she was on a big lumbering ferry—like a humongous barge, with a kids' playroom off in one corner. The ferry was slowly, torturously creeping out of port. Now, with the kids much more independent, she's starting to have sailing dreams again.

As for myself, whenever I become involved with a new group of people, I start dreaming about my old volleyball buddies. In these dreams I'm a teenager wondering whether they'll pick me for the Labor Day V-Ball Tournament. All my worries about being included, all my pride in having a place on the team, is constellated again and I seem to relive the agony and ecstasy.

Everyone has signature dreamscapes and recurring images. Some people dream again and again of baroque architecture, or of wild cats, or of busy cleaning women. Some people continually dream of the people in their office, their old boyfriends, their pets. Sometimes the variations on the imagery last weeks or months; other times they last a lifetime. Following the twists and turns of these sequences of images can often give you insights into what's going on in your psychic life.

In *The Wild Place*, Susan Thompson's dream series about her pregnancy and giving birth, there are suggestive correlations between some of the dream images and what might have been happening to Susan in real life at the time. In one dream, for instance, her husband is nonchalantly burning down the house while she takes care of the children. She also dreams of a woman with a little zipper pouch on her belly out of which she pulls, not a baby, but a tiny woman, full-grown (*see* p. 172).

In another dream series, the exact source of the image transformation is less obvious but still compelling. After my father died, he would appear in my dreams for many months either sick or dying. Then one night I had a dream in which he was well. I knew that he had died but he seemed healthy and vigorous in this dream. My mother was with him and she, too, seemed young and full of life. When I woke up, I knew intuitively that something had changed. My dream mother and father were healthy again. Some grieving process had played itself out. What it was, precisely, I didn't know; but I was sure something had shifted, as if a weight had been lifted.

Similarly, I recall one period in my life when I had dreams that took place in claustrophobic enclosures. The dreams were dark and the atmosphere oppressive. Then one night I had a dream that I was in a brick octagon with eight portals boarded up with bricks. It began to rain. I could hear the rain pattering on the roof. The rain dissolved the bricks that were boarding up the doorways. Out of these doorways marched a parade of people whom I understood represented the human races or the "family of man." I joined them and escaped my prison. Immediately after that, my dream life left enclosures for a series of adventure dreams. Something in me had opened up. I had a feeling of moving forward in my life even though I had no distinct impression in which direction I was going.

When you come across recurring images, then, ask yourself whether the images are the same as before or have changed. If they've changed, you might want to ask if there's any corresponding shift in your real-life circumstance or your emotional barometer.

Dreams, though, are not telegrams from the unconscious, messages from the inner depths. Image transformation is often enigmatic, contradictory, and inconsistent. Yet, taken over time, you can frequently see in the shifting landscape an evolution of new images, a reversion to old images, and a transformation of central themes.

Because people are rarely studious about writing down and remembering their dreams, many dreamers remain unaware that there is such a thing as a dream series or recurring images. Yet this is the aspect of dreams that is most likely to help someone connect the progression of their dreams to the evolution of their waking life. To become more sensitive to this evolution, it may help, when writing down dreams, to make a list of key people, places, and actions. That will make it easy for you to go back over your dream notebook and find affinities between recurring dream images.

Below is an example of a dream series with an evolving image. In this sequence, Anna, a Swiss woman, dreams of different kinds of bulls. The first dream she had around the time of her marriage at age twenty-six. She always remembered it vividly. It was brought back to mind by a series of bull dreams she had in her forties, at a time when she and her husband were deciding whether or not to try to have a child—something they had avoided up until then.

Anna's Bull Series

The White Bull and the Boy

I am walking in the field when I see an enormous white bull with huge horns. (As a child I was always scared of bulls when I would walk along the paths.) The bull corners me against a fence and I know it is useless to run. My husband is beside me and I think we are both going to die.

The bull comes up to me and speaks to me, saying: "Since you are so scared I'll put you over the fence." And very gently he lifts me over the fence and places me down outside the field.

I look back and in the place of the bull is a tall handsome boy of twenty. Somehow I know he is my son. I know he is studying physics at the university. I know everything about him.

Then I wake up.

The Blond Bull and the Ancient Language

I am walking with my father over wide sandy hills, like the rolling countryside of Tuscany. There are a lot of cows in the fields, and at the end of the hill I see this big blond bull. And, of course, I am very frightened and I try to hide behind a barn. But the bull has seen me and comes towards me. But he keeps his distance. So I am not so afraid.

He looks straight at me. Then he begins to speak. "*Grüezi, Grüezi,*" he says, the Swiss greeting: "Hello." And then he says something very clear, like one clear sentence . . . But, oh, I wish I could remember exactly what he said, but I can't. This makes me so sad.

I only remember two things:

He was speaking in some old language, Hebrew or Sanskrit.

And he was saying: "I can transform myself!"

Then he vanished and over the field where he had been standing there was a beautiful atmosphere or aura, like a very light smile.

The Black Bull and the Church

In this dream, I am back in the rural town where I was born. In the field, I see some black bulls, bright black, with a blue glimmer, like Spanish bulls, not big, but finely shaped.

One of them, when he sees me, tries to come through the fence. I think: "Oh no, not again!"

The bull crashes the fence and chases after me. I run to the graveyard next to my house and jump onto a high gravestone. My husband is next to me, but he stays on the ground below the gravestone.

Somehow, the bull finds me, as if he is unconsciously bound to me. When he sees me, he steps over all the old graves in the graveyard, very close to me. To chase him off, I try to throw something at him. Stones, perhaps, or sand. I don't remember what I threw exactly but this was new for me—throwing something at a bull.

It doesn't affect him, though, not really. He doesn't go away. He just stands there staring, staring up at me, perched on the gravestone, so fearful of him, and at my husband down below, helpless before him.

Then something changes—I throw a stone at him, or something, and the bull starts to leave, heading towards the church. I look over at the entrance of the church and see: a priest. The bull has transformed into a priest.

The Brown Bull and the Kiss

Last night, I kissed a bull! A young, curly haired brown bull, like those little Galway bulls. He lay on his backside, and I next to him, and I scratched his breast. He was very peaceful, like a big bear, but it was a bull, and I wanted to come closer, but then I was afraid because of his horns, that he could suddenly jump up from his peaceful position and be a wild animal, throwing me off.

But he didn't. He just lay there.

And I . . . I wanted to lie on top of him. Yes, I did. I was only scared because of his sharp horns! I have to admit, it was very erotic.

Then, ohhh . . . I felt the dream vanishing, slipping away. But before this could happen, I kissed him! I kissed him somewhere on his forehead, near his mouth. I can't believe I kissed a bull!

And then I woke up.

By the time this dream series ended, Anna and her husband had decided to let nature take its course and to try to have a baby.

Creating the Dream Script

The frame image

A frame image is an image that is given special prominence to emphasize a key element or home in on the essence of a dream. It is an image that either repeats itself many times with variations, or an image that is sustained throughout part of the narrative. Like a picture frame, the frame image contains and focuses the rest of the dream.

For instance, in a dream about being chased through a bad neighborhood you could narrate the whole dream while running. In a dream about flying over your old neighborhood, you could narrate the whole dream while flying. In a dream that takes place at a drunken party, you could tell the whole dream drunk.

What makes this technique magical is the ability to sustain the frame image while still making all the necessary transformations to play all the characters, environments, objects, and actions in the dream. In the dream of being chased you have to transform into the stalker, the old men sitting on the stoop, and the trash in the alley while still running in place. In a dream about flying over your old neighborhood, you have to transform into your mother, your dog, the girl next door, while holding your arms out in a flying pose. In the dream of the drunken party, you have to transform into the deejay, the cop at the door, the couple kissing in the corner, while maintaining an alcoholic stupor as if a drunk were telling the dream.

Almost anything can be a frame image: putting a key in a lock, heavy breathing, an evil smile. Whatever it is, it should be central to the emotional heart of the dream, and flexible enough that you can still enter all the other images in your narrative.

Often in a dream that has a strong central character other than yourself, you can use that character as a frame image by making him the narrator. In a dream about meeting a werewolf in the supermarket, for example, you can tell the whole dream in the body and voice of the werewolf. In a dream about running into an old, wise hermit in the forest, you can tell the whole dream as the sage.

Sometimes, a central action can be used as a frame image. In a dream about being eaten alive by ants, you might start the narration unobtrusively scratching yourself now and then as you set the scene. The ants have not appeared yet in the dream, but already, as narrator, you are starting to feel them crawl and bite. This frame image anticipates the climax of the dream and makes the audience wonder why the performer seems so itchy. By the end of the dream, to their horror, they will find out.

You might even frame your whole dream in a style that seems appropriate to your dream. A dream that takes place mainly in a rock club might be performed as if you are in a rock video. A dream that gives you super powers might be played like an action movie. The purpose of these frames is not so much to entertain the audience (though the styles *are* entertaining) but to give the audience a greater sense of what it felt like to be inside the dream.

Frame images, however, are not just useful in holding the emotional center of a dream; they are also essential in simplifying the narrative. In putting together a dream series, so many images are evoked that, even with judicious editing, the audience is in danger of being overwhelmed by image overload. For the sake of clarity, audiences need a frame of reference; and for the sake of drama, they need to know the focus of the action. The frame image—whether a character, an environment, an object, or an action—gives the audience a clue as to what is most important in the dream.

Here's an example of a dream best told through the filter of a frame image, in this case, the image of a lioness. It is excerpted from Susan Thompson's dream series about birthing and nursing her babies. Susan, the performer, goes in and out of the Lioness body and voice even when playing other characters; and she stalks the audience while telling the dream, even when she is playing characters other than the Lioness, like "Peggy," her labor coach. It's as if the image of the Lioness is superimposed over the rest of the dream. By telling the story through the filter of this image, she gives the audience a visceral sensation that the Lioness is everywhere, stalking the neighborhood. By playing all the parts through this filter, she also gives the impression, without saying it in so many words, that she herself has a Lioness inside her.

Susan's Lioness Dream
from *The Wild Place*

Lioness (*stalking the audience*): In this dream, I'm getting into my car and Peggy, my labor coach, is there and she has that no-nonsense look on her face.

I say: "Peggy, what's wrong?"

And she says: "Shut the door."

(*She makes a gesture like a streaking animal.*)

Whoosh!

(*Dropping out of the Lioness image*)

Susan: What was that?

Peggy: Don't panic. It's only an animal.

Susan: I look in the rear view mirror . . .

(*To the audience*)

What kind of animal would hang around this neighborhood?

Peggy: Haven't you heard? There's a lioness in the neighborhood.

(*She gestures like a lioness showing claws.*)

Lioness: And she pulls down her shirt and there, on her shoulder, are these awful claw marks.

(*Dropping out of the Lioness image*)

Susan: Oh my god! Peggy! (*Pause*) Suddenly I think of Stephen, my husband. Where is he? I have to warn him.

(*Giving Peggy's response through the image of the Lioness*)

Lioness: Don't worry about Stephen, woman! He's having a midnight rendezvous with the lioness down by Crystal Lake. She's offering to suckle him and he's crazy enough to do it.

(*She acts out the Lioness offering to suckle him, then drops out of the image.*)

Susan: Then I think: wait a minute . . . Crystal Lake? I was in that neighborhood this spring when the lilacs were in bloom.

Lioness: I was rolling naked in the green grass under the moon.

(*She rolls on the ground like a lioness, then drops out of the image.*)

Susan: I had no idea there was a lioness in the neighborhood. She could have mauled my kids!

And then suddenly I'm out of the car, and I have to get a pizza and some ice cream for dinner.

(*She sneaks away like a lioness in tall grass.*)

Lioness: And I'm very aware that there's a lioness in the neighborhood.

Susan: Maybe I should go back to the house . . . ? (*Pause*) Hell, no, this is my neighborhood. And I've got to get food for my family.

(*Like a fierce lioness*)

Lioness: And suddenly I have a weapon in my hand, a pair of boleadoras, and I feel her presence, watching me, stalking me . . .

(*To the Lioness*)

You better not mess with me. I don't want to hurt you but I will.

(*As the Lioness*)

She's crouching low in the bushes. She's about to spring. I can smell her funky breath and she can smell . . .

Susan: My milk! She smells my milk!

(Like wild animals they circle each other)

Lioness: She backs off. *(Pause)* I back off.

And the whole way back to the house, I can see her shadow out of the corner of my eye. And I know she's got me in her sights. But she knows I've got her in my sights.

(The two wild animals continue to stalk one another from afar. Long pause. She drops out of the Lioness image.)

Susan: And then I'm home.

Combining images

Christopher: *I've got rat dreams. I've got dreams of mongrel dogs, dog turds, dog feces. Dreams of mangy cats scratching pus from my sores. Dreams of a weasel, that I had a weasel for a pet. I even dreamed I got herpes. Herpes! I was happy to get herpes. I was delighted to get herpes. Hooray for herpes! I didn't mind that at all!*

—from *Dreaming with an AIDS Patient*

Often in a long, involved dream series certain kinds of images will repeat themselves with significant variations. For instance, in *Dreaming with an AIDS Patient* it seems important that the image of Marilyn Monroe, the star, the elevated Queen, evolves over time into images of women who are much more down to earth. This has symbolic importance for Christopher, the dreamer, who has strong associations with both earth/mother figures and homosexual "queens."

However, some repetitive images are more significant for their consistent similarities than for their transformative variations. A gnawing rat in one dream might be so similar to a gnawing weasel in another dream that you might make them into a single rat/weasel character. Roses in one dream might be so similar to lilacs in another dream that you might want to choose either roses or lilacs, but not both, to keep the flower imagery focused.

In the Lioness Dream above, Peggy, the labor coach, appears as a strong, competent woman giving advice. Indeed, throughout the dream series in *The Wild Place*, various strong competent women appear who seem like guides, Peggy being the most prominent among them. A decision was made, then, to call *all* of the woman dream guides "Peggy" in order to make the "guide" character clear to the audience and well-defined.

Another way to underline the connection between like images is to cast the same actor in all the similar roles. In Christopher's dreams, there is a sly, shifty character who insists on extracting a heavy toll from him. He is purposely described as a "weasely guy" to connect him to the weasel/rat dreams; but more importantly, he is played by the same actor who portrays the filthy, infectious beasts.

In *Crossing the Waters*, an ensemble's collection of dreams crafted as a soul's journey, one of the unifying images was that of a river. In one early dream, there is a pure, clear, sensuous river. Later, there is a polluted river with a dangerous rusty nail at the bottom. In the last dream, the river is teeming with people swept by a storm—an apocalyptic image leading back to a pure stream. In all these dreams, the same actress portrayed the river even though only one of these dreams was her own. By making her the "voice" of the river, the audience could better follow the transformation of the river imagery.

Finally, affinities and contrasts between dreams can be implied by transforming an image in one dream into an image in another. In *Crossing the Waters*, a house is invaded and the family destroyed by the King of the Rats. Then, in the next dream, the dreamer is the chief of an African tribe who has her head chopped off by the evil Chief of an opposing tribe. In weaving these together, it made aesthetic sense to have the Rat King transform into the evil Chief, as if the Rat King's destructive energy had spilled over from one dream to the next.

Taking poetic license

Throughout this work on Dream Enactment, we have held to the central goal of shaping the work to enable the audience to experience our dreams the way we dreamt them. This, however, has often meant taking certain dramatic liberties with the dream material: stylizing the action, for instance, to capture its essence, adding language to animate inanimate images, including associations and biographical history to create a context, as well as other devices to bring the impact of the dreams home to the audience.

To create a full-length dream show, even more creative horses need to be harnessed to unify the work, focus the image through-lines, and clarify the dramatic transformations. In other words, you have to take a certain amount of poetic license to help the dream series make thematic sense and have a dramatic shape. Poetic license doesn't mean, however, that you make things up or falsify the dreams; rather, you change and transform non-essential details in order to clarify and amplify the major themes and images.

For instance, in *Dreaming with an AIDS Patient*, we chose to emphasize, for dramatic purposes, the contrasts between the two main characters—Robert, the psychoanalyst, and Christopher, the analysand. Christopher is portrayed as very outgoing, sensual, and emotional; Robert is portrayed as much more contemplative, cerebral, and cautious. In real life, however, the person who Robert is based on has a very outgoing, sensual, and emotional side to his personality. But by emphasizing the aspects of his character that are different from Christopher's, it becomes much more moving to witness their growing affection for one another and how they bond together.

Here are some other examples of taking poetic license.

+ Combining three fierce dog images from separate dreams into the image of the three-headed Cerberus, the dog guardian of Hell.

+ Eating a pomegranate in a very ritualized ceremony to emphasize its connection to Persephone, who was doomed to spend half her life in the underworld after eating that fruit.

+ Borrowing matter-of-fact words from one dream—"all my doors and windows were open"—and using them to describe a sexual, emotional state in another dream— "all my doors and windows were open."

The most essential way to take poetic license, however, is by editing, cutting, and simplifying the dreams. Every dream show must do this to some extent. If all images are given equal weight, then no image stands out. If every twist and turn of a dream is included, then often it's impossible to see any through-line at all. The audience simply becomes victim to image overload.

There is a danger to this, however. Indiscriminate editing can alter the essence of a dream, and the inappropriate amalgamation of images can lead to a manufactured interpretation. Like anything else, taking poetic license is an art that should be used in service of the dreams and not as an excuse to make some artificial collage of images.

The purists among us can take comfort in the fact that the mere *telling* of a dream already takes poetic license with the material since the words we use are not the experience itself but a verbal recreation of the experience. We are always adapting, generalizing, editing, and speaking metaphorically in order to get at the truth of our experience.

Making music: the emotional journey

Collections of dreams defy traditional dramatic forms. Even with a personal dream series, it's very hard to string together a dramatic through-line. There may be dramatic conflicts within a dream, but rarely any kind of plot development from one dream to another. Instead, a dream series tends to suggest at best an unfolding of character; a group conglomeration of dreams tends to suggest, at best, a collective worldview. The art of making these shows theatrical, again, is to string together these dreams more like a musical composition than a melodrama. It is the emotional ups and downs, darks and lights, agitations and calms that clue the audience into the shape of the image transformations.

For this reason, the most potent weapon in your arsenal for shaping a dream is sound and music. Even if there was no music in a particular dream, the place, the time, the style, and the mood of it can all be evoked by the choice of sound. Not only can it help you transition from one place to another, sound can also provide the emotional underpinning for the whole dream series. In *Dreaming with an AIDS Patient*, the main character, Christopher, is often seeking a spiritual release from his strict religious upbringing. We chose to embody this through a gospel singer who provides an ecstatic underpinning to the play. The gospel singer eventually enters the play as the image of a minister who, in real life, helped Christopher study for the ministry. But the gospel sound, which pulses through the dream show, is mainly a theatrical device to give shape to the spiritual journey, with songs like these:

Jordan's river is deep and cold
Chills the body, but not the soul.

Deep river,
My heart is over Jordan.

Over. Over.
My soul looks back in wonder
My soul looks back in wonder
How I got over.

If you are making "music" out of dreams, then the order in which you put the dreams becomes very important. Do you put three funny dreams together to make a comic build? Do you put three sexy dreams together to make a sensuous collage? Do you follow a trajectory from joyous dreams to sad dreams or vice versa? Is there a natural shape to the collection of dreams? And if so, where are the climaxes? Where are the turning points?

In the collective dream show, *Crossing the Waters*, we shaped the piece as a downhill slide from sensuous colorful underwater dreams to bloody murderous at-death's-door dreams. In the end, though, there was a series of travel dreams that suggested a soul's journey back from the dark to the light. Charting the course of this soul's journey became the main playmaking challenge and the main principle behind the selection and editing of dreams.

As with any play, a dream show has to take the audience on an emotional journey, a roller coaster ride of evocative narratives and images that transform, develop, and resolve with a sense of harmony or dissonance. To sustain this roller coaster ride, you have to be particularly sensitive to the transitions between dreams. It is in the transitions that the audience becomes aware of whether one dream is an extension of the mood and theme of the previous dream or if it's a change of mood and theme.

In *Dreaming with an AIDS Patient*, Christopher has a dream of marathon runners staggering across a finish line. In the next dream he continues to stagger, having dreamt of a woman who "falls into the drink." In fact, in real life, he has been overwhelmed by the "marathon" of medical treatments and has started to drink heavily (even though he has been warned not to drink while taking the drug AZT). What's important here is the creation of a section of dreams where Christopher is staggering, out of control.

Most important to musical unity are images that tie the dream series together thematically. In *Crossing the Waters*, one of the unifying principles was an opposition between sweet, nurturing images and rotten, destructive ones. That principle, sort of like a yin-yang process, was introduced in the prologue to the play and provided a tension of opposites. These opposing musical harmonies played themselves out through the course of the dream series.

Meghan's Cookie and Apple Dream

(Washed in light, Meghan opens a cellophane package.)

Meghan: For as long as I can remember, I dream of a sugar cookie and a rotten apple core.

(She removes a sugar cookie from the wrapping.)

I see a sugar cookie. It is beautiful and bright. It is very pure and exudes light. I see it either on a simple white plate or suspended in the air.

(She holds the cookie up to the light.)

I know what its exact opposite is. It is a rotten, skinny, pointy apple core. Everything around it—though nothing is around it—I know is dead. The apple core is not infectious but lives somewhere with lots of other things rotten and dark.

(In shadows on the other side of the stage, a dark figure bites into an apple.)

These two—the sugar cookie and the apple core—I know are the most opposing forces in the world.

(She takes a bite of the sugar cookie. The dark figure takes another bite of apple.)

I'm not crazy about sugar cookies, but I buy them more frequently than a person who doesn't really like sugar cookies would. At this point in my life I much prefer apples. It is not the images themselves that overwhelm me but the fact that they constantly change from one to another.

(She crumbles the cookie back into the cellophane wrapping.)

Just like the rotten apple core is destined to morph into the cookie and vice versa, I feel I am destined to always be a witness to it. That joy will become horror, that horror will become joy.

(The dark figure tosses the apple core on the floor and exits.)

I have a headache right now just thinking about this.

Through the Mirror of Dreams

Reliving the dream in rehearsal and performance

There are many different kinds of rehearsals. Some are designed to work on the staging of the action, and some are designed to explore the emotional underpinnings of the characters and images. Sometimes you work on the outer form of the presentation and sometimes on the inner content. In both instances, it's possible to try to go to a deeper level in the exploration of a dream. When you are working on the outer form, you can try to craft with increasing precision exactly what an image looked like and how it sounded. When you are working on the inner content, you can try to find the source of the feelings and the associations that go with them.

Don't try to do both at the same time. It is often difficult to work on emotional material while staging a scene, or work on the technical aspects of a particular movement when exploring a painful or ecstatic moment. However, it's through the exploration process of rehearsal that the layers of the dream unfold and the impact of the images is re-experienced.

You will find, though, that there will be many moments in rehearsal when new things happen that didn't occur in the first telling of the dream. Particularly in interactions with the ensemble, you'll find you have new impulses towards the characters and images in the dream. As in any theatrical production, you have to learn to use your intuition to trust authentic impulses—in this case, ones that are born out of the dream material—and to reject inauthentic impulses that are merely theatrical devices. This is easier said than done. The only criterion you have to go on is whether or not the new impulse helps others dream your dream.

Inevitably, the rehearsal process will change your relationship to your dream. No matter how scrupulous you are about returning to your original narrative, the act of playing inside the dreamscape will alter your perception. Often, the rehearsals become more vivid and emotionally charged than the original experience. You may even discover things about your dream that were completely hidden to you upon first telling. You have to assume, though, that these changes come out of the fabric of the dream. If they feel authentic and help to bring the audience closer to the essence of the dream, accept them and incorporate them in your presentation.

This is particularly true of new discoveries that happen in performance. The presence of an audience is a powerful thing. Suddenly, you have to convey to real people what really happened to you in your dream. Things that seemed obvious in rehearsal are no longer obvious, and things that seemed moving and powerful may fall flat. Moments that seemed serious or painful may elicit a laugh of recognition, and moments that seemed trivial or ordinary may be deeply moving to people who are hearing them for the first time. As in any theatrical performance, the actor must adjust and incorporate the reaction of the audience and learn to communicate with them on an ever-deeper level. At the same time, impulses to play for the laugh or to puff up the melodrama of a moment must be resisted. The art of acting in performance, with dreams or any other material, is to stay alive to new discoveries while remaining true to your basic text.

Moreover, the presence of the audience changes the experience of the dream. The dream is no longer a private affair but something shared. Whether you are performing your own dream or someone else's, its shape will be subtly altered by the response you get. Hearing laughter across the footlights, or seeing tears in the front row, affects your relationship to the imagery. You begin to see emotional moments—painful, sexual, scary, or tender—not only from your own perspective, but also from the perspective of outside observers. This is natural and similar to the experience of actors in any scripted play. Seeing ourselves inside and outside simultaneously is sometimes humbling, but often enlightening.

Dreaming the dream on

Because theater puts you physically inside the dreamscape, it is possible to navigate within it. This gives you an opportunity to identify new details about the dream and to allow the space to incubate your feelings. Beyond this, though, there is a potential to interact with the images to discover more about your relationship to them. This may entail doing things in the theater space that may have only been implied in the actual dream.

If a dark figure is chasing you in a dream, it's possible in the theater space to turn around and face him. If a sick cat is lying on the ground, it's possible to approach and pet her. If there's a mysterious bottle on the kitchen table that's enticing you, you can open it and drink.

This is a form of active imagination. It requires the actor to be fully present inside the dream, and capable of following her impulses wherever they may take her. It doesn't work if the actor forces the story or preconceives what's supposed to happen. When approached spontaneously and intuitively, this improvisation may uncover feelings and associations that weren't obvious in the initial telling of the dream. You discover new things about yourself through the mirror of dreams.

Jerry's Ice Woman Dream

Across the room, on a bed with gold filigree, is a beautiful woman encased in ice.

In performing this dream, Jerry knew vaguely that this woman was scary; but the exact nature of his fear was unknown. In playing with this image, he found himself moving closer to the ice. As he did so, it began to give off, in his imagination, smoke. He realized that the ice was "dry" ice, and that if he touched it he would be burned. The insight that he was afraid of being burned triggered an association with a recent relationship, in which he had been "burned" by a jilting girlfriend when their relationship "dried up." It was this fear of being jilted, specifically, that was encased in the ice with the beautiful woman.

This kind of imaginative insight can help define and dramatize images in rehearsal. A distinction, though, should be made in performance between what actually happened in the dream and what was imagined as a potential but unrealized action. Don't hesitate, for instance, to make the distinction clear in the narrative by saying things like: "When I woke up, I realized . . ." or "She didn't say anything, but I imagined she was thinking . . ." or "It never touched me, but I knew if it did . . ."

Dreaming with the audience

It is a natural temptation, in creating a Theater of Dreams, to want to use the dreams of the audience. It's likely that many members of the audience will be delighted to have their own dream experiences elevated to the level of performance. This can be done by inviting audience members to come up to a mic in the front and tell their dreams. They will perform them naturally without any coaching, in the manner people do when telling dreams around the kitchen table. Alternatively, if time permits, you could try to interview the audience members privately, asking them questions to get them deeper into the imagery and their associations to the dream in preparation for an ensemble recreation of their dream later on. The one thing I would caution against, however, is spontaneously mounting a presentation of the dream on the spot in the manner of improvisational theater. This kind of instant theater tends to trivialize the dreams. They become merely amusing. It tends to emphasize weird or funny juxtapositions rather than the depth of feeling connected to the images.

A simple antidote for this superficiality is to give the audience's dreams enough time to incubate. By culling the dreams a day before they are presented, or at least as the audience is coming into the theater, you can give yourself enough time to get to the depths. I have found that I need at least a half hour alone with the dreamer, away from the intrusion of the audience, to begin to home in to the heart of the dream. Asking audience members in some small way to "savor the nectar" or "salt the wound" of a dream is a tricky thing and requires a lot of tact. Usually, though, people like to go deeper into their emotional lives and will be grateful for the chance to re-experience their feelings before presenting their dreams to strangers.

One of the great attractions of Dream Theater is its deep connection to the audience's own experience, its universality. Even if you don't use actual dreams from the audience, by reminding them of their own dreams, your performance enables them to reconnect to the breadth of imagery and passion they encounter every night. Asking them, perhaps at the start of the show, to call out or write down a key image from one of their own powerful dreams may be enough to stimulate their self-reflection. You might even find a time during intermission to ask them for the "title" of some of their dreams.

"Buried Alive"

"The Sticky Icky Birthday Cake"

"The Horse with the Flaming Hooves"

"I Said: Don't Ever Do *That* Again!"

Then, if you take them on a dream journey rooted in your own personal experience they will recognize themselves in the mirror of your dreams, and their own dreams will become more self-reflective.

The self-reflective dream

Often in waking from dreams we recognize the real-life experience that caused us to call up a particular image in the night. The real-life moment informs the dream and helps us feel the resonance of the image. Sometimes, though, just the opposite occurs: we discover things about our real-life experience by suddenly recalling a dream image that seems to shine an illuminating light on that moment.

This is part of the magic of Dream Theater, sometimes its most dramatic magic: the mirroring quality of dreams. Sometimes dreams give you insight not just into your dream life, but your waking life as well. Below is an example of just such a mirror dream in which the dreamer, in real life, recognizes herself in its self-reflective surface.

Susan's Zipper Pouch Baby Dream
from *The Wild Place*

Susan (to the audience): Right around the time my first baby is due, I dream I'm standing on a tarmac of an airport with all these little propeller planes, and I'm trying to find a flight home.

Suddenly, I see my mother. And she is very pregnant. She's ready to pop. I run up to her and say: "Mother, you're a tub! You're too far along. They'll never let you fly!"

She turns to me and lifts her skirt. Lifts it up over her belly. And there, just below the belly button is a zippered pouch. And I'm really embarrassed but I can't resist. I zip open the pouch. And I reach in and pull out the strangest little baby. She looks like a woman, a perfectly formed full-grown woman, with breasts and everything, only tiny and skinny. She's very white and wrinkled as if she's been in the water too long and she has little crusty sleepers in her closed eyes. And I wipe away the sleepers and rock the poor thing.

(Music: The Skye Boat Song)

I turn to my mother and she's gone. And I've got this thing—this tiny woman baby. And I think . . .

(Pause)

What am I gonna do with this baby?

(Pause)

A few weeks later, in real life, I'm a tub. I still haven't had my baby. I'm twelve days late and I find myself lying in Newton Wellesley Hospital with an I.V. stuck in my arm and a fetal monitor strapped across my belly.

(Sound of the fetal monitor)

But I don't care. I have my candles, my crystals, my labor coach, my pillow, my husband, and a birth plan a couple miles long. I'm listening to a tape of panting meditations and imagining my cervix opening like a lotus flower.

(Fetal monitor slows and stops)

But then the monitor starts to slow down and stop.

I turn to Peggy, my labor and delivery nurse, a tough Irish woman: "Peggy! What's happening?"

Peggy: Susan, stand on your head!

Susan: What?

Peggy: Stand on your head!

Susan: Now Peggy is an ex-nun, married to an ex-priest, mother of five children, so when she says, "Stand on your head" you stand on your head.

(Standing on her head, talking to the baby)

C'mon baby, c'mon baby, c'mon baby, c'mon baby . . .

(Monitor starts up)

The monitor starts up! (*Triumphantly*) Come on baby!

Susan: Immediately, Peggy checks me out. She looks me in the eye and says:

Peggy: Susan, I've been twenty years in labor and delivery and this is not a baby's head.

Susan: It's like a line in a horror movie. "Not a baby's head?!" What the hell is it? Oh my god, what?

Peggy: Susan, calm down! There's a fibroid tumor the size of a pineapple blocking the baby's way out. You're gonna have a C-section.

Susan: A C-section! I start to cry. I've never even had my appendix out.

Peggy: Susan, look at me! Why are you crying? You're gonna have your baby in twenty minutes. Twenty minutes!

Susan: And Peggy's right—twenty minutes later, I'm holding our baby boy, and he's fine. Beautiful and fine.

(Holding her belly)

But later that night, lying there with my belly stitched up with those staples they use, it looks kind of like . . . kind of like a zipper! I remember the dream I had about the pouch-pocket baby. And I'm back on the airport tarmac trying to find a flight home. And I really, *really* want my Mom.

The Theatricality of Dreams

Implications for theater training

I hope it is clear by now that you don't need formal acting training to create Dream Theater. Everyone is an actor and since dreamers are the experts on their own dream experiences, they can act, direct, and write their own dream scenarios with great authority.

At the same time, it should be noted that Dream Enactment is a great tool for theater training. The personalized subject matter, along with the imagistic and narrative challenges, provides an opportunity for both training in theater fundamentals and advanced performance techniques.

By embodying dreams, actors have to use all their physical and vocal skills to capture the nuances of the experience. They have to deal with the personal implications of the dreams, the sensual quality of the environments, the psychology of the characters, the physicality of the actions, and the implied style of the dream story. When practicing in a group for presentation, the actor is also obliged to deal with the ensemble, to relate to the audience, and to use the space effectively. By experiencing these challenges in rehearsal and performance of their dreams, actors become more specific in their choice of action, and more profound in their emotional expression with any script they are asked to perform.

Training the collaborative director

Dream Enactment is a laboratory for collaborative playmaking. Each dream has to be explored by the ensemble, and the dream series has to be ordered in a sequence that makes symbolic, aesthetic, and narrative sense. The director in charge of this process cannot create Dream Theater on her own; she has to rely on the personal discoveries of the dreamers and the improvisations of the ensemble.

Still, like most collaborative ventures in playmaking, Dream Theater needs a director's vision to give coherence and focus to the whole. This is done most effectively not by imposing choices on the work, but by developing them in an organic way. For the director, Dream Theater is a laboratory for practicing the art of "rotating" leadership.

Collaborative playmaking relies on an instinct for knowing when the actors should take the lead in exploring the material, when the playwright or scribe should take the lead in editing the material, and when the director should take the lead in shaping the material. In practice, the leadership can "rotate" between actor, director, and scribe many times in the course of a rehearsal period and even many times within an individual rehearsal. In some ensembles, the distinction between director, actor, and playwright can be productively blurred by having each member of the group take on these roles at different times. Still, in terms of the type of work that needs to be done, distinguishing between the exploratory work of the actor, the editing work of the writer, and the shaping work of the director is important. And it is the director's job to get the timing right. With this in mind, Dream Enactment can become excellent practice not only for making plays based on dreams, but for plays based on any material that is generated collaboratively.

Training the playwright/scribe

The hardest thing for many playwrights to learn is how to make people sound like real people. Often words on stage sound like they are written rather than spoken, as if plays were literary events rather than flesh and blood actions. Dreams are a laboratory for the spoken word, the authentic gesture, and the natural action. By watching and listening to people tell their dreams, playwrights can shape scripts that reflect the way people actually talk and behave. They see, by listening to dream narratives, that often sentences are left incomplete, phrases are repeated, logic is thrown out the window, body language substitutes for verbal language, subtext rides under what is consciously revealed, and emotions are reined in tightly or gush forth uncontrollably.

What's more, every narrator has a unique voice. The distinct style of narrative is a window into the dreamer's personality. Scribing a dream, then, becomes an exercise in shaping a personality. This is good practice for developing distinctive characters in fictionalized plays. It also is a step towards developing one's own voice as an artist. Sounding like oneself is a difficult thing to do.

Most of all, dreams provide a context for watching how human beings display their passions. By listening to dreams, a writer can become a voyeur on a huge range of experiences from the most mundane to the most bizarre. He can hear how people actually experience their lives and describe their feelings, and can witness the power that the imagination plays in everyday life. His writing becomes inspired and honed by observation.

Training through image acting

Dreams, as a treasure trove of vivid, varied, personal imagery, provide actors with a venue for practicing the craft of image acting. Because the imagery in dreams is so vivid and often so divorced from a logical or coherent story line, it easily becomes the foundation for the acting work in Dream Theater. Moving from image to image—that is, following an image score—allows actors to be specific, precise, and emotionally grounded in their dreams. It also provides directors and playwrights with a technique for capturing the emotional and symbolic content of their work in strong, active choices.

This facility for image acting has great practical value in every acting situation whatever the play's style or genre, because everything you do on stage creates an image, a stimulation of the audience's imagination. Gesture, posture, vocal rhythm, vocal quality, movement through space, manipulation of props and costume, relationship to light, and, of course, articulation of language—all of these tools of the actors' trade—create dramatic imagery. You cannot say a line or make an entrance across the stage without creating an image.

Some images, though, are better than others. Some images are deeper, more complex, more metaphorical, more resonant than others. Conversely, some images—like smoking randomly on stage, or pointing without purpose out of habit—can be shallow, messy, unspecific, or crude. By working intensely on images through dreams, the actor can learn to create images that are appropriate to whatever text is at hand. By practicing the art of crafting an image score, the actor can learn how to be present in the moment, moving from image to image in any kind of play: *The Three Sisters, The Tempest, Death of a Salesman, Angels in America.*

This can be a great benefit in moving from rehearsal to performance. Often actors will find their way into a script through psychological or personal connections to the material. They will figure out what makes their character tick and how they would relate to a dramatic moment if it were happening to them. But this is not what they should be thinking about on stage in performance. Nor should they be thinking about the playwright's literary devices or the director's vision. They should simply be playing the moment. One of the ways to root oneself as an actor moment-to-moment is to create an image score, which reflects your rehearsal process. A good image should not only be multilayered in terms of the script, it should incorporate as well all the relevant input from your weeks of exploration and discovery.

An image score is a tool for synthesizing exploration and discovery into playable actions. It is applicable to any style or genre of theater. It is a technique for actors to express their own aesthetic approach to a role, and for directors and playwrights to embody their visions in resonant actions on stage.

The Dream Café

So: imagine a nightclub—small round tables, low light, candles—and up where the jazz band would play there's a stage. On that stage a troupe of actors appears for late-night dreams. A soundman with a synthesizer sits off to one side and starts tolling a bell. The Dream Show is about to start.

For the next forty-five minutes, the troupe will present a set of dreams like a set of jazz with themes woven together through image and narrative like some kind of theatrical music. The troupe takes a break and over good wine or strong coffee members of the audience, stimulated by the dream set, share their own reminiscences of dream life. The bell tolls again and a second set of dreams is enacted. Maybe even some dreams culled from the audience are presented as an encore.

This is one vision of a Theater of Dreams: a place where actors and audience re-experience their dreams. The style would not be dreamy, but precise. The goal would be to have the audience dream the actors' dreams. The breadth of experience that we all possess in dreams—what I call "Our Own Shakespearean Stage"—would be revealed. Actors and audience would come together in a world of imagination where the fantastic and the mundane sit side by side and our passions are unleashed in the most ordinary circumstances. Here we feel the overlap of our dreamscapes with our waking life, and we leave the theater feeling that our world is much fuller than we usually allow.

The magic of a dream show is that it's essentially autobiographical, a true personal story distilled and embellished by the creativity of the dreamer's dream weaver. The Dream Café demands a commitment to be true to the dream story, while crafting a theater piece that resonates on a more universal level. This is an attempt to stretch the boundaries of contemporary theater by throwing our intimate, personal, imagistic experiences on a larger archetypal canvas.

All the trappings of the stage—sound and music, dance and movement, sets and lights, props and costumes—are brought to bear on making the images vivid. All the techniques of playwriting—dramatic builds, character revelations, plot developments, and the like—are considered in making the characters and the actions come to life. Most of all, we find the dramatic event within each dream and, where possible, the resonance between the dream images and real life.

Take, for example, the following scene from *Dreaming with an AIDS Patient*. This is based on a pivotal dream that revealed to Christopher an important aspect of his sexual orientation, and revealed to his analyst, Robert, how their formal relationship had become more intimate.

Christopher's Eight Ball Dream
from *Dreaming with an AIDS Patient*

(We hear music with a heavy disco beat.)

Christopher: So, when the weather bloomed this spring, and I was feeling stronger, I started going to The Eight Ball. The Eight Ball is a dance bar and I go there regularly to be with men, and I don't do anything dangerous with them afterwards, but I dance and we dance and it's nice.

(The Male Brawler & Female Brawler[10] enter and hit on Christopher.)

Male Brawler: Hi there?

Female Brawler: Hey, good lookin'.

Christopher: So in this dream, I'm on my barstool at The Eight Ball writing in my dream notebook, when this . . . this "man" comes up to me.

(The Brawler speaks in his ear, seductively)

Male Brawler: Rough olive skin . . .

Female Brawler: Curly, dark hair . . .

Male Brawler: European looking . . .

Female Brawler: Jewish looking . . .

---

10. Notice that both an actor and an actress play "The Brawler" to represent the masculine and feminine sides of this dream figure, and that the audience is used as the crowd on the dance floor of the dream.

Male Brawler: Not your type.

Female Brawler: Not your type.

(Music changes to a slow romantic melody.)

Christopher: But he's wearing this rose in his lapel—like the roses outside Robert's office—and for some reason I'm very attracted.

Male Brawler: Everybody's very attracted . . .

Female Brawler: Men and women—he's really hot!

(They both start dancing with Christopher, slow and sexy.)

Christopher: So I start to dance with him and we dance real slow, and we dance real close.

Brawler Male & Female: Real slow . . . Real close . . . Kissing . . . Kissing . . .

Christopher: And suddenly we're kissing—we're kissing passionately. And I'm all excited kissing him. I'm all aflame, when . . .

(Pause)

Suddenly, I realize—

(Music stops abruptly.)

This is a dance floor. You can't do that here.

(Christopher looks around very embarrassed. Brawler Male & Female approach the audience provocatively.)

Male Brawler (*to the audience*): Hey, get your face out of my face!

Female Brawler (*to the audience*): Haven't you ever seen a kiss before?

Christopher (*to the Brawler)*: Don't make a scene!

(The Brawler strikes taunting sexual poses in front of the audience.)

Male Brawler: You love it and you know it.

Female Brawler: You look so good in red.

Christopher: But he does stir it up. I mean, this guy is a brawler; he just eggs them on. He pricks them and needles them and teases them like crazy. They

get hotter and hotter, and he loves every minute. He's having a ball brawling.
So they start shoving, he starts shoving. And just as I think the crowd is gonna
cream this guy, I realize . . .

(Pause)

Man, he's charming the pants off of everybody.

(The Brawler taunts the audience.)

Male Brawler: At least you're breaking a sweat.

Female Brawler: At least it's not bor-ring.

Male Brawler: Dance?

Female Brawler: Wanna dance?

Male Brawler: Well, I'm gonna dance . . .

Female Brawler: I'm gonna dance . . .

Male Brawler: —and if you want to stand there gawking at me . . .

Female Brawler: —well, you can just stand there gawking at me.

Male Brawler: But why don't we all just have a good time!

Female Brawler: Why don't we have a good time!

(Music starts up again with a heavy disco beat like Janet Jackson's "Nasty Boys.")

Christopher: How does he do it? I don't know. He pushes and shoves and blusters
and brawls and just when everyone gets red hot, he turns it on and cools them
out. And that's what he calls a par-tay!

(Music rises. Lights fade on the dancers in silhouette. Christopher dances alone.)

And watching him "par-tay" in my dream, I suddenly saw . . . I saw . . . How can I
say this? I saw that he's a *man*. That he's a *real* man, but at the same time very
feminine. And it hits me—I mean it is just so clear—that there's a great difference
between wanting to *be* a woman, and wanting The Woman to come *through*
you, wanting The Woman to be *alive* in you. Do you know what I mean? I mean
this man really *moved* me.

(Sound of ticking clock. Dancers fade. Lights transform to Robert's psychotherapy office.)

Robert: And the atmosphere in my office is really charged! And we never actually talk in session about how this nightclub brawler seems to look like me: European looking, Jewish looking. And I never point out that another place kissing is not supposed to be allowed is in analysis with your analyst. Or that the analytic relationship is like a dance on the dream floor where we ball and brawl to get to know everybody. We never discuss it. But it's in the air. And I know, and he knows, and I know that he knows, and he knows that I know . . .

(Long Pause)

And that's when I think we fell in love.[11]

Some Dream Theater Images

from *The Dream Project,* Brandeis Theater Company

Photos on the following pages are from *The Dream Project,* which was produced and performed by The Brandeis Theater Company, Waltham, Massachusetts., April 19–29, 2007. The show consisted of two one-act dream plays—*The Monkey King Dream Cycle* and *Sara e Salvo*—created in collaboration with the actors using their own dreams. The acting ensemble here consists of Brandeis University graduate actors Ramona Alexander, Naya Chang, Matt Crider, Lindsey McWhorter, Sara Oliva, Joshua Davis, Robert Serrell, Anthony Stockard, Brian Weaver (Heather Klein, stage manager). Special thanks to Managing Director David Colfer for permission to use the company's photo gallery. All photos by Mike Lovett.

---

11. This is a dramatic recreation of a dream presented in analysis. For the actual texts of Christopher's dreams, and a full description of the personal and analytical relationship, see Robert Bosnak's book, *Dreaming with an AIDS Patient* (Boston & Shaftesbury: Shambhala, 1989).

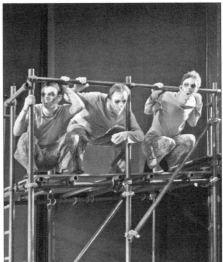

Dream Characters: Masks and stylized movement create the Monkey King (left) and his monkey entourage (right).

Dream Environments: The men portray a fierce and indifferent sky; the women, a seething earth below.

Dream Object: A hub cap and a rolling chair create a wild and comical runaway car that is doomed to crash.

Dream Action: Star-crossed lovers say their reluctant goodbyes.

Dream Ensemble: A childhood dream is created by surrounding a young girl with all her toys, seen here behind her.

Part Four

WAKING DREAMS

Dream Enactment in Daily Life

Flying into Moscow, 1991

August 19: Gorbachev ousted; tanks roll into Moscow.

August 20: Yeltsin defies coup; crowds defend barricades.

August 21: Coup fails; celebrations in the street.

Dreams have given me lots of insights over the years: insights about my inner landscape, about my life's journey, about what makes me tick. But of all the insights, the most powerful has been the notion that we are all dreaming while awake.

By this I mean that our dream maker, our image-maker, our imagination, is always turned on, not just at night. We imagine our lives even as we experience them. We resonate with the images of everyday life on an emotional, intuitive, symbolic level. We ask of every moment, "What's it like?" We don't notice this because there is so much else going on, so much "reality noise" drowning out the imagery; but the imagery is there nonetheless, and we feel it.

This was brought home to me most vividly when I found myself, by chance, flying into Moscow on August 19, 1991, the day Mikhail Gorbachev was ousted from power by a neo-Stalinist coup. As we drove from the airport, the tanks were grinding down the ring road outside of Moscow towards the center of the city. On the outskirts, we passed the memorial to where the Red Army stopped the Nazis on their push towards Moscow in World War II. In our conference center, we tuned in to Radio Moscow for news until the government clamped down on it; then we tried to tune in to CNN until the government clamped down on that; and then we were under the iron hand of censorship. I found myself living in a dream of World War III.

In so-called "reality," I had flown into Moscow to do a workshop in Dream Enactment at the invitation of Robert Bosnak, who was organizing the first dream conference of its kind ever held in Russia. The point of the conference (among other things) was to consider the interface and interaction between one's "personal unconscious" and the "collective unconscious." We could not have asked for a better laboratory. While our personal reactions to the crisis bubbled up, the collective unconscious of the Muscovites was spilling out onto the barricades.

What dreams we had, both sleeping and waking! Some of us were caught up in a dream of liberation, like the French Revolution. Others were caught up in a dream of gulags and concentration camps. Still others, lubricating themselves with shots of vodka, treated it like a spectator sport in a banana republic. As for myself, with two small children back home in the U.S., I was caught in the dream of the End of the World, melodramatically wondering how I was going to survive the chaos that could devolve into the Third World War.

Of course, you could describe these different reactions from a psychological, or political, or cultural point of view, showing how different people react differently to the same event. But in this case I think it would be much more accurate to say that the different reactions were fueled by the different images we had of this event—that is, from the waking dreams we constructed in our imaginations.

Since that time, I have been keenly aware of how even ordinary events— making a presentation at a faculty meeting, playing catch with my kids, being stuck in a traffic jam—are loaded with imagery and symbolism. If you simply ask yourself, "If this were a dream, what dream would I be in?" the emotional resonance of daily life can hit home.

It has often been said that there is no such thing as an archetype, just specific examples of it. The spirit of Aphrodite is constellated in the intimate laughter of your lover; the spirit of Ares appears in the blood bonds of two soldiers in the trenches; your Shadow lurks in the face of that derelict who leers at you from an alley. Daily life abounds with archetypal imagery, which, if we tune in to it, amounts to a waking dream.[12]

With practice, dream work can change the way you look at your life. You can experience it through imagery, your own personal imagery and the collective imagery that is all around us.

---

12. The term "waking dreams" is borrowed from the title of an excellent book by Mary M. Watkins on active imagination (Dallas: Spring Publications, 1984).

For instance, at this moment I am both writing this section and dreaming that I am writing it. The one who is merely writing it is focused on the task at hand. The one who is dreaming it has a much richer experience. On one hand, I am reminded of the image of my father who was also a writer. On the other, I'm feeling oppressed as if I'm locked in my college dorm room, chained to my desk to finish a term paper. Some inflated part of me sees myself in the presence of the pantheon of dream writers like Freud and Jung. And some inferior part of me sees myself as a hack newspaper reporter banging out a thousand words to fill a deadline. The image of writing this section resonates on many levels if I just tune out the static of everyday life and listen to the music of my dream maker.

You yourself undoubtedly are dreaming right now as you read this book. If this is a dream, what dream are you in?

What's that like?

Life Dreams

We are such stuff as dreams are made on

When we see a jet trail high in the clouds, a dream of foreign adventure may be constellated. When we see a woman in a red dress on a balcony, a dream of romance may be born. When we catch the eye of that crazy old lady on the subway, a death dream may be stalking us.

Imagery is everywhere. Our hearts and minds respond to images in real life just as they do in dreams. The material is similar. It is *all* imagination. It is through our imaginations that we experience the story of our lives.

Our imagination—our inner image-maker—is turned on all the time. We don't turn it off when we wake up. On the contrary, it's our constant companion. All the sights, smells, sounds of everyday life have both a literal connotation and a symbolic resonance. It's often hard to recognize this because our minds are so busy, so preoccupied with waking consciousness, that our imaginations are drowned in mundane static. Besides, there's so much we have to do just to get through the day that it's hard to focus on our dream weaver. We tune out the emotional overtones generated by daily images though we feel them, nonetheless.

The smell of bacon in the morning brings us back to Sunday mornings when we were very young; the evil look of the bus driver fills us with paranoia and dread; the sight of a handsome young man dandling an infant may lead to longings for marriage and family. If we treat these as dream images, our emotional reactions to daily events become more acceptable, more enjoyable, more creative.

It takes practice, though, to recognize the imagery of everyday life; this is where the telling of dreams can be helpful. It trains your eye to identify images. The acting of dreams is even more helpful because it trains not only your eye, but your body as well.

Dream Enactment is a discipline, then, for recognizing imagery. It creates a sensitivity to moments in your life that have a dreamlike quality. You see a sickly, emaciated man in the supermarket and feel how under-nourished you are in your own work. You see a bright yellow dress in the store window and are brought to tears remembering your mother in her youth. You take a friend from out of town for a tour around your city and are filled with the excitement of a foreign adventure. These associations are waking dreams.

Often, waking dreams go unrecognized because the real-life context overwhelms the images. We scratch the surface of the moment and simply say to ourselves (if we say anything at all): "What a sick old man!" "What a pretty yellow dress!" or "What fun to show my friend around." We forget to check in with the personal feelings we are having or the associations, fantasies, memories, and metaphors that are evoked.

Here is an example of an unexpected, waking dream that surprised me at a meeting in an office:

Waking Dream of Baby in the Budget Meeting

I am sitting in the budget meeting of the board of directors of my kids' Charter School, when the president of the board, a woman who has recently given birth, excuses herself from the weighty deliberations to nurse her baby. All of us on the board know one another very well, so it's not surprising that she stays seated in her presidential chair while lifting her loose blouse to give suck to her infant. We go on with the meeting as if nothing is happening and, of course, avoid putting the spotlight on her during this intimate time. And yet, the cooing baby is so satisfied and the beaming mother is so content that everyone at the meeting, I believe, is enchanted by the waking dream of Madonna and Child. We may be dreaming different versions of this dream depending on our associations with mothers and babies, but the image of the nursing child is so much stronger at that moment than the image, say, of the budget from the Long Range Planning Committee that you would have to say we are more present inside the waking dream than inside the budget meeting.

Inscape and instress

Life, like dreams, has no obligation to be meaningful, purposeful, or coherent. But, like dreams, it often seems as if it is. We often feel that things happen for a reason and that life makes sense. When this is not so—when we feel that random events are driving our lives on a chaotic journey leading nowhere—we often feel that something is wrong, that things ought to happen for a reason, and that life should make sense. Despite evidence to the contrary, most of us carry within ourselves a sense that life has, or ought to have, a shape. Human beings seem to have built into our psyches a shape maker, a kind of "life artist" that creates connections between disparate moments in our lives and finds meaning in the patterns.

But how can we tune in to our shape maker, our life artist?

In his famous poem, *Pied Beauty*, the poet Gerard Manley Hopkins pulls together a collection of objects and experiences which are "pied"—that is, multi-textured—and sees in them a reflection of the glory of God in all His multi-textured facets. To describe his creative process making poems, Hopkins uses two words, "inscape" and "instress." In shaping his poetry, "inscape" is considered like an inner landscape, a tapestry of disparate things that intuitively seem to belong together in a unified whole. "Instress" is like the inner "stress" or feeling that binds these things together and gives a sense of wholeness to the tapestry. Hopkins' inner landscape of variegated things, his "inscape," gives rise to his inner feelings, his "instress," of the glory of God.

I find these terms helpful not only for the making of art, but for viewing life in aesthetic terms. They help identify the working process of our dream weaver, the one who creates not only nighttime dreams but waking dreams as well.

In real life, if we take the time to notice our inscape, we sense a connection between many different things that happen to us. A chance encounter on a plane, a passage in a book, a heartfelt talk about relationships, might all seem to be connected somehow. Similarly, if we think about our instress, the inner feeling that sums up our emotional journey during the day, we can sometimes look back over the events, the inscape, that caused those feelings: the plane, the book, the talk.

A headline in the newspaper about polio in Africa, the approach of the anniversary of your mother's death, a lecture at work on time-management, a farewell dinner for a friend going abroad, and the Beatles' song "In My Life" heard on the radio may all hang together in some sort of associative quilt about time and mortality. A ride in a new car, a picnic with your sweetheart, a poster for Air India, and the smell of French bread might bring up feelings of restlessness and wild urges for adventure. In each case, an alternative series of events or encounters might weave an entirely different inscape even on the same day. In other words, your life may have many different shapes depending on how you put the collage together. Each of these collages is a waking dream.

You know your inscape, the inner landscape of your waking dreams, by following the associations that come up when you monitor your feelings. Conversely, you know your instress, the feeling of being inside your waking dreams, by sensing the events that seem to give shape to your life.

The difficulty in sensing our inscape on a daily basis is that in our minds we tend to put things together logically rather than intuitively. The difficulty in sensing our instress on a daily basis is that we tend to keep our feelings at bay just to get through our busy day. In order to alter this state of affairs, all we need to do is look for the patterns of our dream weaver, and tune our inner antennae to the symphony of feelings that exist every moment, every day, and in the course of a lifetime.

Pied Beauty

Glory be to God for dappled things—
　　For skies of couple-colour as a brinded cow;
　　　For rose-moles all in stipple upon trout that swim;
Fresh-firecoal chestnut-falls; finches' wings;
　　Landscape plotted and pieced—fold, fallow, and plough;
　　　And all trades, their gear and tackle and trim.

All things counter, original, spare, strange;
　　Whatever is fickle, freckled (who knows how?)
　　　With swift, slow; sweet, sour; adazzle, dim;
He fathers-forth whose beauty is past change:
　　Praise him.

—Gerard Manley Hopkins

The waking dream diary

Like the practice of remembering dreams, the practice of recognizing your waking dreams becomes easier the more you do it. If you take a moment every day to make a shopping list of the key moments in your day, you'll begin to recognize patterns. You don't have to *try* to make patterns; patterns will simply emerge. This is the function of your dream weaver, the image-making faculty you have which is associative and intuitive rather than rational. When starting out, be sure not to limit your daily "experiences" to what you do; include the experiences of what you feel, think, and imagine. If the sight of a heavy snowfall reminds you of a brutal passage in Jack London's *Call of the Wild*, the harsh experience of the wild huskies is as much a part of your inscape as the beauty of the new fallen snow. If the smell of coffee in the morning reminds you of how much you miss your mother, then your instress includes your grief over her passing. If a headline about starvation in Africa recalls a deeply felt urge to drop out of the rat race and do something worthwhile for a change, then that, too, might become part of your waking dream.

By following your feelings, associations, intuitions—the instress of your day—you can construct on a daily basis a new kind of diary, a record of your daily inscape experiences; in effect, a waking dream diary.

To view your waking dream diary, you might want to start a real-life image score, not unlike the image score you made when enacting dreams. This would be a list of images that tracks the events so that, like a nighttime dream, your waking dream can be reconstructed as both a narrative and as a collage. Fleeting impressions—a headline in a newspaper, a rude remark on a bus—can be given as much weight as a business plan you presented at work, or a long argument you had with your teenage daughter.

The important thing is to be aware of how themes run through your day; how the moments connect or contrast to one another. Try not to force the themes or the connections. Assume rather that the waking dream already exists and that you are merely clearing away the mists of daily busy-ness to see the emotional, imagistic fabric underneath.

For instance, yesterday happened to be my son Jonah's seventeenth birthday, June 12. On the same day, my friend Stan, a jazz musician, came to visit. Simultaneously, my wife, Kanta, and I divided up the chores to get the birthday together. She bought the cake and I picked up the last present, an electric guitar. Memories of the actual birth day seventeen years ago came back. There was a sense of time fleeting but also a remembrance of new life springing up in June. Tensions around getting chores done mixed with celebration.

But this is *not* the waking dream. This is a recitation of major events of the day, with a suggestion of the themes. The waking dream was much more specific, being made up primarily of images. Here are a few of them associated with themes of Birth and Death.

Waking Dream Diary: June 12

Birth images

- Image of the golden chain tree in the yard (Jonah's birthday tree) dripping with golden blooms

- The oozing, sensuality of Death-by-Chocolate cake

- Memory of Jonah's wet, pointy head when he was first born

- Ritual family recital of Jonah's first song: "Summertime"

Death images

- Stan's story about the time he almost drowned in Hawaii

- Stan, Kanta, and I all on low sugar/starch diets: sugar as the enemy

- Toilet backing up; mildew smell in the back hallway

- Jonah singing Grateful Dead songs on his new guitar and my fantasy that he will be singing them after we are long gone

Contrast images/the daily grind

- A long and petty argument over who would pick up the birthday cake

- News that the new dishwasher is coming tomorrow, thank goodness, dishes piling up

- Jonah's stress over his homework assignment, a personal essay: "What is a good person?"

- Stan's corny musician joke to Jonah: "So, how do you get to Carnegie Hall? Practice, practice, practice."

These are only some of the images, a few among many that had immediate emotional impact. And this is only one of many waking dream patterns that could be made out of the same day. In practice, the most important patterns will rise to the surface, allowing the others to recede into the background. If kept up over a period of time, you will discover from the waking dream diary that most of your personal issues, private longings, and profound insights crop up every day. These are the underpinnings of your image life in daylight. Keeping a daily image list with accompanying memories and associations will help the weave of these waking dreams become apparent.

Waking Dream Exercises

What movie are we in?

Here is a waking dream exercise anyone can do, anywhere, anytime. Having lunch with a friend or a close colleague, ask yourself: "Is this person like my brother, my rival, my lover, my confidante? If we were in a scene from a movie, what kind of movie would it be? And which movie star would play my friend? Which movie star would play me?"

You can do a similar imagination exercise at a boring meeting at work or school. Ask yourself, if this meeting were not about the stated subject—the budget, say, or the school picnic—but about the feelings or undercurrents that are lurking beneath the surface, what would this meeting be about?

At a party we often do this exercise without even knowing it. We size up who we are interested in and who we want to avoid; who is trying to make themselves the center of attention and who is hanging on the periphery; who reminds us of an old flame and who reminds us of an old enemy. We just don't call this a waking dream exercise. We assume it's just normal social interaction, rarely stopping to realize that many of these reactions are fueled by our projections onto the real life images.

So, riding on the subway or waiting on line at a coffee shop, look at the person next to you and ask: "If this were a dream figure, what kind of dream figure would he or she be? What would I want from this dream person, and what would he or she want from me?"

The power of projection

Here is another exercise to get in touch with your personal imagery using the power of projection in a group. Sitting in a circle, look across at a person opposite you and ask: "If this was not my friend or colleague but someone from my past, who would it be? If this was not my friend or colleague but someone from my future, someone important in my future, who would it be? If this person were not a person at all, but a creature in the wild, what creature would it be? If she were a force of nature? If he were an alien from another planet?"

By simply asking the question, creating the category for your imagination, you will automatically project an image onto the person. You can do a similar exercise with landscapes you are passing in a train: "If I lived there, who would I be?" Or objects on a dressing table: "If this ring had a magic power, what power would it have? This comb? This pill?"

This is a particularly good way to flush out the preconceptions you have about people, places, and things as well as your fantasies, prejudices, and desires towards them.

The ten-year troupe

Taking this a step further in a more elaborate exercise, you might create a whole scenario about each person in your group by imagining you know them all intimately over a long period of time. This works particularly well if you do it when you are first starting out together, before you actually know too much about one another.

Look around the circle of new faces and imagine that these strangers are actually members of a troupe of actors that has been together for ten years, traveling all around the world, presenting classic and contemporary dramas. Imagine that this troupe works as a collective so that everyone not only acts in the plays but performs some other necessary task for the collective, like doing publicity, or building sets, or fixing the bus when it breaks down. What's more, since ten years is a long time, everyone in this troupe has had lots of interactions with everyone else: some are involved romantically, some are rivals, some are best buddies, and some bitterly estranged.

Looking around the room, then, using your imagination your dream weaver, let yourself "dream" about these people. You might even put it in cinematic terms, creating a scenario for a movie about this acting troupe—

starring, of course, yourself. Ask yourself first of all: "What roles do I and the others usually get in the repertoire of plays?" In other words, how are you and the others typecast? Who always plays the ingénue, who plays the gangster, who plays the noble king, who plays the clown? And in the children's shows, who plays the fierce lion, who plays the wise owl, who plays the beautiful bird, who plays the sly fox? Project onto the people in your new ensemble what type of person they are, even though you know almost nothing about them.

At the same time, ask yourself what tasks each person might perform in the theater troupe, thinking as much about the affinity they might have for their imagined job as the skill it requires. The person who always makes the travel arrangements might seem to have an exacting and orderly persona; the person who builds the sets might seem to be someone who likes to get down and dirty. The person who always buys the booze might be a wild guy, or the one who needs to drown his sorrows. This may be a little harder to do than typecasting, but it will require you to project onto each person a practical action in the real world.

Finally, ask yourself what your relationship would be to each person. Who do you secretly admire? Who would you hate to be stuck next to on a bus for twelve hours? Whose shoulder do you cry on? And who betrayed your trust?

The important thing is that you do this exercise before you actually know too much about all the people in the group. If it is truly to be a reflection of your dream weaving ability, you need to let your imagination and not your real-life interactions lead your fantasies about these people. Later, when you get to know everyone much better you'll probably find that some of your intuitions about each person were uncannily correct while others were dead wrong. In either case, you'll be able to see the power of your imagination to create images even while awake.

The 24-hour drama

An extension of the waking dream diary—the 24-hour drama—can lead to a theatrical presentation of your waking dreams. It is adapted to dream work from an exercise in playwriting suggested by performance artist Spalding Gray, whose monologues are, in many ways, great examples of waking dreams.

The goal is to create a theater piece out of your experiences in the twenty-four hours just before coming to your rehearsal, class, or workshop. It works best if the task is sprung on the ensemble without any forewarning, so that the twenty-four-hour period is free from self-consciousness.

Unlike the TV show 24, this drama is non-fiction. The theater piece will be created out of patterns that emerge in the twenty-four-hour period, those that cohere and those that contrast. In keeping with the idea of following your instress to find your inscape, these experiences should include not only your activities but your fantasies, memories, and associations. In other words, you are going to find the shape of a "day-in-the-life," using the associative connections to make meaning out of the seemingly random events of the day. For most people, any twenty-four-hour period contains the seeds of most, if not all, of our major life issues. The microcosm of a single day often mirrors the macrocosm of our life's journey.

Turning these connections into theatrical images creates a performance piece very similar to a dream presentation. To develop the work, you can use the same steps you would use for Dream Enactment. Start by exploring the events and images of real life without using words, only body and voice. Then tell a partner the key moments using words, while still physicalizing all the images and playing all the parts. Tell it again with a Q & A session to get out all the details. Then edit and shape the material for solo performance, or show the material to a small group to develop it further into an ensemble piece.

For actors, directors, and playwrights, the 24-hour drama is a powerful exercise for practicing the development of plays through improvisation and collaboration. It is also an intense venue for re-experiencing the imagery you encounter in real life and a strong tool for honing your sensitivity to the waking dreams that enrich your life every day.

This exercise can be adapted for any period of time: a week, a year, a lifetime.

Lucid Dream/Lucid Life

Waking into dreams

On occasion, when we dream, we find ourselves aware that we are dreaming. These lucid dreams can be incredibly intriguing, sometimes delightful, sometimes disturbing. Sometimes they give us control over what we are dreaming. Often, though, they give us control only over what we want to have happen and not necessarily what actually happens.

In these circumstances, they bring us to a realization that dreams are an alternate reality as vivid and solid as our waking life. They are very useful to dream work in so far as they give an unmistakable impression that dreams have their own integrity. People and creatures in dreams do not think they are dreaming. They have their own concerns and desires. They do not obey our commands or follow our wishes unless they choose to. They have an independent existence. This realization is helpful in getting out of our own point of view and seeing the dream world through the eyes of the other characters.

There is a down side—the negative side—of lucid dreaming, though, that has the opposite effect of reinforcing an egocentric point of view. The allure of lucid dreams is that, if you know you are dreaming, maybe you can control the dream; maybe you can walk through it and do whatever you want to do, call up whatever image you want to call up, or take any action without impunity. After all, it's just a dream!

In practice this rarely happens, because as soon as you try to impose your will on a dream it usually evaporates. Nonetheless, books and dream gurus who advocate lucid dreaming often tap into this narcissistic impulse, undermining the thing that's most appealing about dreams: they are not our ego's tool.

If you don't try to control them, though, lucid dreams can be very useful in cultivating the ability to be awake and aware in the midst of your experiences. It can be as simple as turning on a self-reflective light bulb in your dream:

"Ahhh, here I am, dreaming." The only thing that has changed is that you are holding up the mirror to your own actions.

This has wonderful implications for your waking dreams. The very act of noticing that you are responding to the images of daily life in the same way as you respond to images in dreams is already a self-reflective act. An even greater act of self-reflection, though, is to take a lesson from lucid dreams and resist the temptation to control the real-life moment simply because you are self-aware.

It may take a lifetime to embrace this discipline.

Below is an example of one of my own lucid dreams, which illustrates the independence of dream characters and the unhappy consequence of trying to control them.

Dream of Questioning Esteban

I am sitting in a local pub, the kind of cheap place that actors hang out in after a show. There is a bar behind me, and little wooden tables in the corner where I am sitting. Theater people I know are milling around behind me, drinking, talking, but I am totally focused on an actress sitting across from me. She has honey-colored hair, big brown eyes, and an enchanting smile. She is a little boyish looking but very attractive. In an earlier part of the dream I had seen her from a mountaintop playing Medea or Clytemnestra in an outdoor arena and I was impressed. I feel she knows and admires my work as a playwright and it is understood as we sit there that we are looking for a way to work together. It is a fact of the dream that her name is Esteban.

Suddenly, I am vividly aware that I am dreaming. I say, "Esteban this is a dream. Right now I am lying in bed and I am dreaming." Esteban looks at me in disbelief, like I must be a little crazy. I take her hand in mine and press it, feeling how warm and moist it is, how remarkably solid for a dream. I repeat, pressing her hand: "This is a dream."

I love Esteban and feel desperate to figure out a way to keep in contact with her after I awake. So I ask her where her theater company is located and she says they have a theater in the Keys, meaning, I suppose, the Florida Keys. Good. This is a start. I ask if she knows any of my former acting students from my university, figuring maybe I can track her down through them? No, she says.

And now she's looking more distressed because she doesn't understand why I'm giving her this grilling. And I am beginning to doubt this reality. So, just to find out if she even exists in my world, I ask her who the president of the United States is. Without hesitation Esteban answers, "Fan Findler." To her "Fan Findler," a woman, is undoubtedly the president of the United States.

The dream begins to fade. Oh, no, I'm losing her! I kick myself for wasting the dream on stupid questions when I could have just enjoyed the company of the enchanting Esteban.

When I woke up, I Googled Fan Findler with no results. I had no associations to the name either. But I did have an association to Esteban. It took me a while, but I suddenly realized that Esteban was Stephen in Spanish, a strange name for a girl. But Stephen was the name of my best friend and musical collaborator, the one connected to my Wild Men Dream, who died prematurely and whom I loved as intensely as I loved the elusive Esteban.

A Goodnight Dream

I said at the beginning of this book that its larger purpose is to reanimate the ordinary through the imagery of dreams and bring the extraordinary back into our lives by acting them out. I also pointed out that, while dreams reflect the mundane details of our daily lives, in them we also share experiences equal to those of the kings, queens, traitors, debauchers, witches, faeries, killers, and innocent lovers of the Shakespearean stage. It seems only fitting, then, to end with a dream that reflects on this very point: the expansive range of our dream lives. Here is the final dream of *The Wild Place* in which Susan's mother tells Susan how to put children to sleep with dream stories.

Susan's Golden Light Dream

Susan: Months later, around the time baby Skye starts eating solids, I finally get my period and have another dream.

(A golden light shines)

In this dream, there's light flooding everything. I'm on a coastline and a boat is coming into harbor. I'm sitting in a very utilitarian building, like a bathhouse. And golden light pours through the open windows.

(She basks in the golden light.)

I have my boys with me, and I've got to put them to bed. And it's not going to be easy with that golden light. But it's not going to get any easier when the sun goes down because then the moon will rise up full to flood those windows in silver. And I better have some really good stories to tell to put the kids to sleep.

(Silver moonlight floods the stage.)

I turn and there's a woman sitting next to me and she has a basket—and it's my mother.

(We hear music: The Skye Boat Song)

And her basket has a zipper, like the zipper pouch on my mother's tummy in the dream on the airport tarmac.

(Sound of airplane propeller)

And I'm not sure I want to look inside this pouch—maybe it would have a tiny woman inside it like the pouch on my mother's tummy—but I . . . I can't resist, and . . .

(Looking inside a picnic basket)

Inside...

(Pause)

There are books . . .

(She pulls out books)

Children's books. But true stories. Stories about real people. The people who live here on this coastline, in this harbor.

And my mother turns to me and says something like:

Mother: Susan, I'm a realist. But all these people here, they're dreamers. I listen to them. They tell outlandish stories to your boys. They call your father "The King." They call me "The Queen." And all the little insignificant details of our lives they make into great adventures and dramatic conquests. But I don't mind because I'm practical. I say, if it works, use it. You see, Susan, this is the way you put children to sleep.

(Opening a book)

With stories like these . . .

(Susan recites The Skye Boat Song as if it is a story from the book.)

Susan (*singing*):

Loud the winds howl, loud the waves roar
Thunderclouds rend the air.
Baffled our foes stand on the shore
Follow they will not dare.

Sail Bonnie boat, like a bird on the wing
"Onward" the sailors cry!
Carry the boy who's born to be king
Over the sea to Skye.

Tho' the waves leap, soft shall ye sleep
Ocean's a royal bed.
Rocked in the deep, Mama will keep
Watch by your weary head.

Sail Bonnie boat, like a bird on the wing
"Onward" the sailors cry!
Carry the boy who's born to be king
Over the sea to Skye.

Index

About the Author

JON LIPSKY is a director and playwright whose full-length dream plays include *Dreaming with an AIDS Patient*, adapted from the book by Robert Bosnak; *The Wild Place*, adapted from the dreams of Susan Thompson; *Crossing the Waters*, adapted from the dreams of Boston University students; and *The Monkey King Dream Cycle* and *Sara e Salvo*, adapted from the dreams of The Brandeis University Theater Company.

Other plays he has written have been produced at the Actors Theater of Louisville's Humana Festival, The American Repertory Theater, The Berkshire Theater Festival, The Merrimac Repertory Theater, La Mama ETC, The Boston Center for the Arts, and other regional theaters. He has been Associate Artistic Director of the Vineyard Playhouse on Martha's Vineyard, where he lives, and playwright-in-residence at The Merrimac Repertory Theater, and TheaterWorks/Boston. In 2007, he received the Boston Critics Eliot Norton Award for Best Director.

Lipsky is also Professor of Theater at Boston University's College of Fine Arts. He introduced Dream Enactment as part of the curriculum of the Theater School's professional training program more than 20 years ago. Since then he has conducted classes and workshops in Dream Enactment at the European Graduate School in Switzerland, the Canadian Museum of Civilizations in Ottawa, the Actors Theater of Louisville, Trinity Square Advanced Actor Training programs, Emory University, Massachusetts Institute of Technology, Emerson College, Oberlin College, and other academic and professional venues.

His early work in dreams involved the study of Embodied Dreamwork with Robert Bosnak, a diplomate of the C.G. Jung Institute and past president of the International Association for the Study of Dreams. Using Bosnak's methods, he led a series of dream groups in the early 1990s. He also led Dream Enactment groups for psychologists at the "Dreaming in Russia" conference in Moscow, and the Jung Institutes in Boston, Massachusetts, and Ithaca, New York.

Currently, he is developing a late-night cabaret for dreams called The Dream Café, produced by The Underground Railway Theater in at the Central Square Theater Cambridge, Massachusetts. He continues to lead workshops in Dream Enactment in Boston and other cities throughout the year.

For information about Dream Theater events and to arrange for workshops or other events in your area—visit www.larsonpublications.com/Jon-Lipsky.